Mexican Cookery Today

Kate Hendry recently travelled around Mexico collecting recipes and observing Mexican cooking methods. In **Mexican Cookery Today** she has adapted Mexico's traditional cooking methods to the modern kitchen, but has been careful to retain the essential ingredients for an authentic Mexican meal.

Mexican food has a vibrant quality: hot, fiery sauces enliven eggs and meats. The addition of chocolate to a chicken casserole at first surprises but then delights by its taste. **Mexican Cookery Today** contains a wealth of exciting recipes which will bring the true flavour of Mexico into your home.

KATE HENDRY

Mexican Cookery Today

MAGNUM BOOKS

Methuen Paperbacks Ltd

A Magnum Book

MEXICAN COOKERY TODAY
ISBN 0 417 03980 8

First published in 1979
by Magnum Books

Copyright © 1979 by Kate Hendry

Magnum Books are published by
Methuen Paperbacks Ltd
11 New Fetter Lane, London EC4P 4EE
Made and printed in Great Britain by
Hazell Watson & Viney Ltd
Aylesbury, Bucks

Contents

NOTE: Unless otherwise stated, all recipes in the book serve 6 people.

Preface by Jack Beeching

Your roast turkey, last Christmas or Thanksgiving, your child's chocolate bar, the tomato juice in your own Bloody Mary – all were tastes on the tongue encountered by Europeans for the first time when the Spaniards landed in Mexico. The *conquistadores* discovered that the Aztecs had a strange and wonderful civilisation – but they also had a fascinating cuisine, using corn, beans and chiles, with a few extraordinary ingredients, like chocolate and tomato, which made the medieval European cookery they were still eating back home taste insipid (at last!).

Mexican dishes still have that vibrant quality – strange, bright, hot, louder and larger than life, like the country itself, with its vast, limpid distances, incandescent sun and smouldering violence. But modern Mexican cookery has been enriched over the years from yet another source. Great advances were being made in cookery in the Europe on which the *conquistadores* had turned their backs, as first the Italians, then the French, discovered the civilised cuisine we now know as a life-enhancing minor art. The essential exchanges between Europe and America soon began. Friars sent Indian corn and tomatoes back home, and brought in those foodstuffs and spices commonly used in Europe which made all the difference, sugar to go with the chocolate, black pepper to complement the red chile. From this fruitful intercourse between two cultures – two great continents – came the modern Mexican cookery you will find in this book.

Mexican dishes are not for the timid. The bland fried egg, as served in that everyday repast, *huevos rancheros*, lurks under a fiery scarlet sauce. The question you are bound to ask when confronted with a not very thrilling chicken in its plastic wrapping, just lifted from the supermarket shelf –

roast? boiled? casseroled? – is answered in Mexico by several dozen chicken recipes, each more thrillingly pungent than the last.

Those who plump up alarmingly on bread may well turn to the crisp and nutty-flavoured tortilla with relief. And let us, for instance, consider the bean, that little, hard, dry vegetable, an incomparable source of protein, which the experienced cook smiles upon indulgently because it has such a happy knack of absorbing and compounding flavours. Beans and Indian corn were, and still are, the everyday diet of the simple Mexican countryman. But long before he was born, Mexican civilisation had set its wits to work to glorify the bean. If your experience has so far been limited to that harmless and nourishing pink comestible tipped out from a tin with the well-known number in so many of the world's furnished rooms, you will here for the first time meet the bean as civilised provender.

Nowadays, in almost every town, those who enjoy good food have discovered for themselves the discerning stores where ingredients at one time impossible to come by are now freely on offer. There you will find for yourself the simple materials of this exotic cookery. Read, shop, cook and, at last, try for yourself dishes which bring a provocative sting to your tongue, flavours which play mariachi music somewhere at the back of your mind. There is no need either, with these recipes, to squat down and slap tortillas from palm to palm, or cook them over charcoal in the back yard. After travelling far and wide in Mexico to observe cooking methods and collect recipes, Kate Hendry, God bless her, has done all our donkey-work for us. She has skilfully and wisely adapted Mexico's traditional cooking methods to the modern kitchen. She has tracked down the valid equivalents for Aztec or Maya ingredients which you are most likely to find in that favourite shop of yours. Her recipes have been tested, verified, simplified. So, even though your first Mexican meal may emerge from an electric oven, and be brought to table on a Wedgwood platter, if you do exactly what Ms Hendry tells you, the smell will be real, and the taste a flavour of an unknown distant land.

Acknowledgements

I should like to take this opportunity to pay a small tribute to Mexican hospitality in general – their international renown in this respect was more than doubly confirmed during our time there – and also to the many friends who helped make this book possible.

Many thanks go to Laura and Oscar Maldonaldo; Irene Dominguez Garcia and her brother, Miguel; Beatriz Medina and her grandmother; Alejandro Ribera Jimenez and his family; Angela and Rolando Castro; Magdalena Mora Vargas; Juana Baez; and to the countless other Mexican cooks who generously shared their secrets with me.

Finally, warmest thanks to my husband, John, who valiantly acted as guinea-pig for four years and is still coming back for more!

Basic Ingredients

Maize, beans and chile are absolute essentials in all Mexican cookery. They feature in varying forms at every meal and, indeed, many Mexican peasants eat very little else. Maize and beans are easily obtainable in Britain and, though you may not find a great choice of fresh chiles, the more uncommon varieties are becoming available either dried or in tins.

MAIZE

Tortillas

¡ *Mas tortillas, mujer, y calientes esta vez!* (More tortillas, woman, and let's have them hot this time!) is a common cry at Mexican mealtimes, which while revealing the notorious *machismo* of the Mexican male also shows the vast consumption of these maize pancakes (up to 20 per person at every meal!), and the need to keep them wrapped in a fresh linen cloth until they are all cooked so that they retain their heat. About six tortillas with the meal would satisfy an average British appetite.

Traditionally, tortilla-making was the major occupation of the women in the Mexican family. The whole day would be spent chatting in the kitchen while this most important task was being performed. The girls were taught from a very early age how to flatten out the small balls of *masa* (dough), passing it quickly from one hand to another with a slapping sound which was to be heard throughout the morning in every household.

One can imagine the signs of relief from the Mexican housewife with a large growing family when this task was taken out of her hands by the local *tortillería*. Large amounts of *masa* are made and fed into a machine which turns out hot ready-cooked tortillas at break-neck speed. The women bring along a fresh cloth to take away the kilos of tortillas required for the midday meal.

Such a modern convenience is not available to us in Britain but it is possible to buy maize flour at good delicatessens (recommended brands are Quaker's *Masa Harina* and *Minza*: see p. 162 for stockists). The tortillas made from maize flour are almost indistinguishable from the real thing, in which the dough is formed from corn kernels and not flour. Here is a recipe for the real thing:

Nixtamal (Tortilla Dough) from Corn Kernels

1 *kg* (2¼ *lb*) *corn kernels*
3 *litres* (5¼ *pints*) *water*
50 *g* (2 *oz*) *lime**

Wash the corn and boil in the water with the lime. When the skins begin to come away from the kernels, remove from the heat and leave to cool. Rub the kernels between the hands until the skin is removed, discard the skin and wash the kernels thoroughly. Grind the kernels to a dough of very fine consistency.

Nixtamal from Tortilla Flour (Masa Harina)

4 *large cups tortilla flour*
2 *large cups water*

Empty the flour on to a large flat board or marble slab. Make a well in the centre and add the water little by little, pushing the flour into the well. When all the water has been

*The chemical, not the fruit. Calcium hydroxide, or slaked lime, is available at your chemist.

added, knead so that it is well mixed. The dough is a pleasure to handle and comes off the hands cleanly as you turn it.

Now that you have made the *nixtamal* by either of these methods, you are ready to form and cook the tortillas.

Tortillas

Shape the dough into balls slightly larger than a walnut. Mexicans who began doing it as little girls can flatten the balls with the hands but you may find that placing the ball between two large flat plates covered with a piece of thin plastic film is more satisfactory. Place the ball of dough in the centre of the bottom plate and press the top one down fairly hard so that the tortilla is as thin as you can make it without breaking. Remove the plate, peel off the piece of plastic and gently pick up the tortilla being careful not to break off the edges. Place immediately on a large pre-heated ungreased frying-pan. The Mexicans use a large flat earthenware plate, a *comal*, for this, on which many tortillas can be cooked at once. A hot-plate is ideal but one or several large heavy-bottomed frying-pans or griddles will serve as well. Cook for 3 or 4 minutes each side, pushing down with four fingers every so often. The sign of a truly successful tortilla and something eagerly looked out for by every Mexican woman is that it puffs up with air when it is cooked. If you can do this, you are a woman indeed and deemed worthy to marry the man of your choice!

Whilst the tortillas are cooking, more balls can be rolled and flattened. When cooked, wrap the tortillas in a clean linen cloth in a basket, piling them up as they come off the heat. A delightful lime smell begins to pervade the kitchen as the tortillas are cooked.

Unless a simply vast quantity of tortillas are being cooked at one time, in which case the bottom ones may have to be popped back on the heat for a minute or two, the tortillas thus stored will retain their heat until they are all ready and the meal can be served.

Tortillas de Harina

Tortillas can be made with ordinary plain flour, though the flavour is not the same. In Mexico City, people always eat *tortillas de harina* with *cabrito* (whole roast kid). Some of the more 'progressive' Mexicans claim they prefer wheat flour tortillas (despite the fact that they have less nutritional value), as maize tortillas along with chile give them indigestion. It is difficult to say how much this is true and how much this is snobbery. You may like to investigate for yourself, though personally I come down strongly in favour of maize tortillas.

1 kg (2¼ lb) plain flour 5 tablespoons lard or other fat
2 teaspoons salt   Warm water

Sieve the flour and salt together. Make a well in the centre and add the melted fat and enough water to make a soft dough. Divide into balls and leave on a floured board for about 30 minutes. Flatten and cook the tortillas as in the recipe for maize tortillas (p. 13).

As well as accompanying every meal, tortillas are used in many dishes such as *tacos* (p. 120), *gorditas* (p. 114), *enchiladas* (p. 107), *quesadillas* (p. 112), *chilequiles* (p. 115), and *pastel de pobre* (p. 47).

Maize is also used in the making of *pozole*, a highly spiced soup-stew (p. 118) and *tamales* (p. 116), a great Mexican favourite generally reserved for fiestas and traditionally requiring hours of preparation.

BEANS

Many different sorts of beans are now available in wholefood shops and delicatessens in Britain. Mexicans like the black bean from Queretero and the Bayo Gordo or pink bean best, though all colours are grown and thoroughly enjoyed.

The black bean is highest in nutritional value, containing

more protein and iron than any other. They give out a very rich and delicious juice. Though black beans are not very common in Britain, some are now being imported from Tanzania; they are worth looking out for.

Beans should be washed and soaked overnight. Place to boil in the same water (you may prefer to change the water as this makes the beans more digestible, though a Mexican would say you are thus losing a lot of the goodness) with a piece of garlic and onion. Cook for two hours in a covered (preferably earthenware) pot. Then add a good lump of lard (about the size of an egg) and continue cooking for another hour or until done. Add salt to taste ten minutes before serving. Beans can be very successfully pressure cooked (about 1 hour) if you are short of time, though you may find the beans are tastier by the slow method.

Beans are eaten with every meal, usually after the meat course with more tortillas and *salsa roja* (p. 128) in small bowls with a wooden spoon. Traditionally, apart from the tortilla and a knife, this spoon was the only cutlery required.

Beans are often served *refritos*. They are mashed and fried up with a little lard to re-heat them. Mashed beans are incorporated into many other dishes, such as *tortas* (p. 120) and *gorditas* (p. 114).

CHILES

If the word *chile* conjures up in your mind a small green vegetable not unlike a tiny green pepper with a smartingly piquant flavour, take a trip one day to the market of La Merced in the heart of Mexico City. There the amazingly wide diversity in colour, shape, size and strength of the chile will be only too evident amidst the noise and clangour of busy tradesmen.

The chile was eaten in America many centuries before the arrival of the Spaniards. Ninety-four different varieties of chile had been identified as being cultivated in Mexico, though sometimes different varieties are known by the same name and sometimes the same variety is known by a different name according to the region which produces and eats it.

Here are the names of the principal types of chile grown in Mexico: ancho, mulato, pasilla, serrano, jalapeño, guajillo, cascabel, piquín or chiltepín, carrecillo, or torna-chile, habanera, cora, guajón, bola, gordo, arribeño, guero, costeño, atotonilco, huachinango, puya, cristalino, trompo, bolita, catalina, ornamental, chile de agua, liso, pinalteco, zacapeño, San Luis, chilaco, loco, chilguacle, chircozle, chiclateco, mihuateco, pimiento, chile de arbol, poblano, chile mirasol rojo and many others of lesser importance. You may be lucky enough to find some of the more uncommon chiles in Britain. The ordinary green chile may be used in most recipes in the book, except when it is stated otherwise. Any type mentioned in the book can be bought either dried or in tins from delicatessens or from the stockists listed on p. 162.

The chile is an essential part of every Mexican meal, either in flavouring soups or stews or in the sauces which accompany it. A delicious combination of chocolate and a carefully balanced selection of different chiles makes *mole*, one of Mexico's most outstanding dishes (p. 58).

Chile powder is eaten on almost everything with salt and often lemon. Try sprinkling chile powder on peanuts or crisps. Sprinkle salt, lemon and chile powder on halved oranges or a slice of pineapple or a mango. Deliciously refreshing on a hot day.

Antidote to chile!

If you make a dish which is too hot for some of your more timid guests, sprinkle a little sugar over it. This takes the edge off the chile.

Whilst maize, beans and chile are essential at every Mexican meal, here are some other useful stand-bys for your Mexican recipes:

CHICHARRON
Crispy Crackling

Chicharrón can be bought at most butchers in Mexico in enormous crispy slabs. Chicharrón frequently accompanies meals when it is eaten with *guacamole* (p. 129), *salsa roja* (p. 128), or used like a tortilla to scoop up beans or meat. It can also be cooked in a spicy sauce.

Chicharrón can be made in a British kitchen and is a pleasant crunchy addition to the meal. Ask the butcher to cut the skin off a young pig for you, with 2 cm (a good half-inch) of fat on it. Score the fat and soak the whole piece in water for several hours. Remove and dry thoroughly with a clean cloth. Heat 8 tablespoons of oil in the bottom of a large saucepan and cover the bottom with the skin, cut into pieces small enough to fit into the pan. Cook very slowly for several hours until the skin becomes transparent. Then increase the heat and cook until the skin puffs up. Place the chicharrón on absorbent paper and serve when it has cooled along with the meal or as a snack, sprinkled with salt, lemon and chile powder.

CHORIZO

Chorizo is a highly spiced pork sausage of Spanish origin often incorporated into Mexican dishes. Spanish chorizo can be bought at delicatessens but it is fun to try making your own Mexican ones, which will taste more authentic and which can be kept for up to a year in a cool, well-aired larder. This is an excellent way of preserving meat.

1 kg (2¼ lb) pork, minced	1 teaspoon ground cinnamon
1 onion	¼ teaspoon ground cloves
6 cloves garlic	Salt to taste
100 g (4 oz) chile powder	¼ litre (½ pint) vinegar
100 g (4 oz) paprika	4 tablespoons vodka
1 teaspoon black pepper	250 g (9 oz) pork fat

Mince the meat, onion and garlic together and mix thoroughly with the spices, salt, vinegar and vodka and the finely diced (to about the size of a pea) pork fat. Stuff into sausage casing and tie off in 10 cm (4 in) links. Leave the sausage to hang in a well-aired place for at least 24 hours, when it can be used, though it is best after a couple of months.

GREEN TOMATOES

Two completely different species of tomato are commonly used in Mexico: *jitomates*, which were introduced into Europe from the Americas along with potatoes and tobacco and *tomates* which are small and green and are surrounded by a waxy leaf. These latter are not easily available in Europe and whilst *jitomates* (our tomatoes) will serve as a substitute, the flavour is rather different, though the firmer and greener they are, the better.

TOMATO PUREE

Many of the recipes in this book ask for tomato purée. This is *not* the concentrated purée you buy in tubes or tins. One cup or a ¼ litre (½ pint) of tomato purée may be made from ¼ kilo (½ lb) of fresh tomatoes. Boil the tomatoes for a few minutes in a little water. Remove the skins, place in the water to boil until they are soft. Cool. Pulverise in an electric blender and sieve. The tomato purée is then ready for use. Tinned tomatoes are generally cheaper in Britain and are just as good. You do not have to skin or boil the tomatoes, just pulverise them in their own juice and sieve to get rid of any seeds. One 200 g (7 oz) tin will make 1 cup of tomato purée.

If you wish to use the concentrated tomato purée, one small tin is equivalent to 1 cup of tomato purée.

CORIANDER LEAF

Coriander leaf, *cilantro*, is a great favourite in sauces and in soups and stews, being rather like parsley with a bite to it. Try growing it in a pot in the kitchen from the coriander seeds which can be bought at most grocers.

Kitchen Implements

Cazuelas and Ollas

Most pots, pans, dishes and jugs are made of earthenware as pottery is one of Mexico's oldest crafts. Some of these have extremely beautiful designs whilst others, though plain, make the kitchen a pleasure to work in because of their muted colours and varied shapes.

Cazuelas or casseroles come in all shapes and sizes but are generally basin-shaped and can be turned to a multitude of uses.

Ollas (pots) are taller with a smaller opening and are excellent for cooking beans, soups, Mexican *café de olla* and hot chocolate.

The Molcajete and Tejolote

One essential piece of equipment is a pestle and mortar which is large enough to grind herbs, chiles, tomatoes and other vegetables. An electric blender may be used but in some cases, the resulting texture may be too smooth. The Mexican *molcajete* (mortar) is generally a three-legged bowl made out of grey-black lava whilst the *tejolote* (pestle) is cylindrical, tapering to fit comfortably in the hand about 10 cm (4 in) long by 5 cm (2 in) wide.

Whilst the Mexican implements are pleasing to look at as well as fitting the needs of the housewife so exactly, it is easy to find a suitable substitute in Britain.

Not so with the *molinillo* (chocolate-beater), which is a special stick, rather like a very elaborate spurtle, hand-carved out of wood with several rings running loose around it. The *molinillo* is immersed in a tall jug (*olla*) containing hot chocolate. When it is rotated between the hands, the rings spin round, causing the chocolate to froth up. This implement is an aesthetic addition to any kitchen but is admittedly not absolutely essential. An egg-whisk would serve the purpose almost as well.

Mexican Eating Habits

Desayuno

The Mexican gets up at sunrise and has a light breakfast before setting off to work, usually *café con leche*, a glass quarter full of strong black coffee topped up with frothing hot milk, and some sweet rolls, *pan dulce*.

Almuerzo

By about ten o'clock, however, he has worked up an appetite and feels ready for *almuerzo*. This is a good and filling meal to keep him going till dinner-time. A typical menu would include fresh orange juice or a slice of water-melon or paw-paw, eggs or steak or meat of some kind, tortillas, beans and more *pan dulce* to finish off.

Comida

The main meal of the day is at three in the afternoon. This generally consists of three courses: soup, either vegetable or a *dry soup* made from rice, macaroni, noodles or tortillas or both if it is a special day, a meat stew with tortillas and beans and a *postre* (pudding), usually fresh fruit or *flan* (crème caramel) or jelly. The meal is generally washed down with a *licuado*, fresh orange, grapefruit, carrot, paw-paw, melon, or strawberry juice, though beer with salt and lemon is found to be most refreshing.

Cena

Supper is a very light meal, usually comprised of a hot milky drink with biscuits or *pan dulce* or a piece of fruit.

Starters

Ceviche Acapulqueño
Fish Cocktail

To see a Mexican man in the kitchen is a rare thing indeed but a few of our male acquaintances proved to be very proficient in the art.

One outstanding example of what can be produced was a simply stupendous meal cooked by the brother of a dear friend of ours, who extended his hospitality to us whilst we were staying in Acapulco. We had been promised fish and I have never tasted any so good. The menu was comprised of *ceviche*, a fish cocktail, *gambas en ajo*, king prawns cooked in garlic, followed by fried *huachinango*, red snapper, served with lemon and a hot sauce. Here is the recipe for the *ceviche*.

500 g (1 lb 2 oz) haddock
Juice of 1 lemon
500 g (1 lb 2 oz) tomatoes
1 small onion
2 small green chiles (optional)
2 tablespoons tomato sauce
1 tablespoon tomato purée
  (p. 18)

½ tablespoon Worcester sauce
100 g (4 oz) olives
Juice of 1 orange
Olive oil to taste
1 teaspoon oregano
Salt and pepper to taste

Cook the fish in the lemon juice over a low heat for half an hour. When cooked, squeeze out the lemon juice and fish stock. Chop very finely the tomato, onion and chile. Add to the fish with the sauces, olives, orange juice, olive oil and oregano, seasoning with salt and pepper. Stir everything well and chill thoroughly before serving in tall glasses.

Aguacates Encamaronados
Shrimps in Avocado

3 *large ripe avocados*	*Juice of 2 lemons*
2 *tablespoons cream*	2 *tablespoons white wine*
100 g (4 oz) *tomatoes*	*Salt and pepper*
150 g (6 oz) *shelled cooked shrimps*	*Chile powder*

Slice the avocados lengthwise, scoop out some of the pulp and mash it with the cream. Chop the tomatoes finely and mix with the shrimps, the lemon juice and the wine. Add salt and pepper to taste. Refill the shells of the avocado with the shrimp mixture. Garnish with the avocado cream and sprinkle with chile powder. Chill and serve.

Aguacates Rellenos
Stuffed Avocados

200 g (7 oz) *peas or green beans*	3 *large avocados*
1 *carrot*	*Oil and vinegar to taste*
2 *hard-boiled eggs*	*Salt and pepper*
1 *green pepper*	100 g (4 oz) *ham or liver pâté*

Cook the peas or green beans (or both, half and half) and the carrots. Chop the white of egg and green pepper. Some of the pepper may be cut in strips and reserved as a garnish. Peel the avocados carefully and cut in half lengthwise: ripe but not oversoft avocados are best for this. Place on a plate and sprinkle with oil, vinegar, salt and pepper. Make the filling with the vegetables and the ham or pâté. Mix well, add salt and pepper and fill the halves of avocado with the mixture. On top of each, put a spoonful of mayonnaise (see p. 131) and garnish with the white of egg and strips of pepper as desired.

Coctel de Camarones
Shrimp Cocktail

2 *small green chiles*
500 g (1 *lb* 2 *oz*) *tomatoes*
Juice of 2 *lemons*
3–4 *tablespoons olive oil*

Salt and pepper to taste
150 g (6 *oz*) *cooked, shelled*
 shrimps

Grind or blend the chiles with the boiled, peeled and sieved tomato. Add the lemon juice, olive oil and salt and pepper. Pour over the cooked, shelled shrimps. Stir well. Chill and serve in glasses over shredded lettuce with salted crackers.

Pâté Especial de Oscar
Oscar's Special Pâté

500 g (1 *lb* 2 *oz*) *pork liver*
250 g (9 *oz*) *chicken liver*
250 g (9 *oz*) *beef liver*
1 *cup breadcrumbs*
4 *eggs*

2 *small onions*
3 *cloves garlic*
1 *sprig thyme*
1 *bay leaf*
Salt and pepper

For the sauce:
2 *cloves garlic*
½ *small onion*
1 *poblano chile*

2 *tomatoes*
Salt

Mince the liver finely and add the breadcrumbs and beaten egg. Chop the onion and garlic very fine; add thyme, bay leaf, salt and pepper to taste and mix all the ingredients together well. Press the mixture down into a well-buttered baking dish and put in a moderate oven, standing in a roasting tin full of water for 1½ hours. Serve hot with a sauce made as follows:

 Grind the garlic with the onion. Add the skinned and

deveined poblano chile and grind well. Finally, add two chopped skinned tomatoes and a pinch of salt. Grind and serve poured over the slices of pâté which should be accompanied with tortillas.

In small portions this may be served as a starter but is also a good light supper or lunch dish.

Apios Rellenos
Stuffed Celery Sticks

A fresh and crunchy start to a meal.

200 g (7 oz) soft cheese	100 g (4 oz) salted almonds
100 g (4 oz) Roquefort cheese	Salt and pepper to taste
4–5 tablespoons fresh cream	2 whole heads of fresh celery
1 small onion	

Mix the two cheeses with the cream to form a soft paste. Mix in the finely chopped onion and the chopped almonds. Season with salt and pepper. Cut the green leaves from the celery and separate the sticks carefully. Leave to soak in cold water for 15 minutes then fill with the cream-cheese paste.

Apios Rellenos de Queso y Pina
Celery with Cheese and Pineapple Stuffing

2 whole heads of fresh celery	1 green pepper
100 g (4 oz) cream cheese	1 red pepper
3 tablespoons fresh cream	200 g (7 oz) black olives
250 g (9 oz) pineapple	Salt and pepper to taste

Wash the celery very carefully. Separate the sticks and leave in cold water with ice for 15 minutes. Meanwhile mix the cream cheese, cream and sliced or mashed pineapple. Use the mixture to fill the celery. Place on a flat platter in the form of a star. In the centre of each stick of celery, place alternately a piece of green or red pepper. Pile the olives in the centre of the plate. An attractive appetiser.

Jitomates Rellenos
Stuffed Tomatoes

250 g (9 oz) peas or green
  beans
1 carrot
1 green pepper
100 g (4 oz) ham or liver pâté
2 hard-boiled eggs

Oil and vinegar to taste
Salt and pepper to taste
6 large tomatoes
100 g (4 oz) mild Cheddar
  cheese

Boil the peas or beans and the carrot and mix with the chopped green pepper, reserving a few strips of the latter for garnish. Add the ham or liver pâté as preferred and the chopped egg white. Add oil and vinegar, salt and pepper to taste.

Peel the tomatoes carefully (this is made easier by dropping them for a minute in a pan of boiling water). Cut a small lid off the top of the tomatoes. Scoop out the seeds with a spoon, leaving only the outer casing. Put the tomatoes on a plate and sprinkle with salt, pepper and oil. Fill them with the vegetable mixture and garnish with strips of cheese and a spoonful of mayonnaise (see p. 131).

Wet Soups (Vegetables)

Soup in Mexico is of two sorts, one the liquid type universally known as soup, the other a *sopa seca* or dry soup made from rice or other farinaceous ingredients which either substitutes or follows the wet soup.

Both types have to be made with a good basic stock, made as follows.

Caldo Para Sopa
Stock

Chicken, meat or fish (chicken feet, meat bones or fish heads serve well if no meat is to be boiled for the meal)
3 *carrots*
1 *turnip*
1 *onion*
1 *small cabbage*

1 *leek*
1 *stalk celery*
6 *black peppercorns*
2 *cloves*
1 *sprig mint (except with fish)*
1½ *litres (3 pints) water*
Salt to taste

Put all the ingredients on to boil, seasoning with salt. The meat or fish which is to be served as the main dish may be used to make the stock. If a fish stock is made, a handful of previously soaked chick-peas may be added. Boil the bones over a low heat for 3–4 hours, removing the meat for the meal when it is cooked. Strain the stock and use for making soups and sauces.

Sopa Mexicana
Mexican Soup

1 *chicken breast*
1 *onion*
Salt and pepper
6 *tablespoons tomato purée*
  (*p.* 18)

1 *tablespoon onion juice*
½ *cup cream*
2 *avocados*
100 *g* (4 *oz*) *cream cheese*

Cook the chicken breast in 3 litres (5¼ pints) of water with the onion, salt and pepper. When tender, remove from the stock and dice. Sauté the tomato purée and onion juice in lard. Add the strained stock and leave to boil for 15 minutes. Remove from the heat. When slightly cooled, add the cream, diced chicken and garnish with strips of avocado and the cream cheese.

Sopa Estilo Puebla
Soup Puebla Style

250 *g* (9 *oz*) *cooked pork*
2 *tablespoons lard*
1 *onion*
2 *corns on the cob or* 1 *medium*
  tin sweet corn
3 *courgettes*
2 *poblano chiles or green*
  peppers

6 *tablespoons tomato purée*
  (*p.* 18)
2 *litres* (3½ *pints*) *meat stock*
Salt and pepper
4 *tablespoons grated cheese*
2 *avocados*

Chop up the pork and brown slightly in the lard. Add the diced onion, kernels of corn, diced courgette, toasted, cleaned and chopped chiles, the tomato purée and finally the meat stock, salt and pepper. Leave to simmer until the vegetables are tender.

When ready to serve, garnish with the grated cheese and diced avocados.

Sopa de Pescado
Fish Soup

2 *large fish heads*
1 *slice lemon*
Bay leaf and thyme
Salt and pepper
1 *leek*
1 *tablespoon butter*
1 *tablespoon lard or oil*

1 *small clove garlic*
1 *tablespoon flour*
1½ *litres (3 pints) milk*
½ *litre (1 pint) stock (in which fish has been boiled)*
1 *cup boiled, chopped spinach*

The fish heads should be boiled with the slice of lemon, the bay leaf, thyme, salt and pepper.

Chop the leek and fry in the butter and lard with the crushed garlic. Add the flour. Before it goes brown, add the milk and the fish stock. Finally add the finely chopped spinach. Allow to boil a little and serve.

Sopa de Camarones
Shrimp Soup

500 g (1 *lb* 2 *oz*) *fresh shrimps*
1 *tablespoon flour*
100 g (4 *oz*) *butter*

1 *tin asparagus tips*
100 g (4 *oz*) *cooked peas*
Salt and pepper

The shrimps should be washed and peeled, and the shells and legs (apart from the eyes which make it bitter) are boiled in 2 litres (3½ pints) water or stock. Sauté the flour in the butter. When it is golden brown, add the stock made with the shrimp shells with also the liquid from the asparagus, stirring well so that no lumps form. Cut up the shrimps and add to the stock along with the asparagus tips and the cooked peas. Season with salt and pepper and add the rest of the butter just before serving.

Sopa Marinera
Soup of the Sea

50 g (2 oz) butter
1 clove garlic
2 tablespoons flour
2 litres (3½ pints) good stock

250 g (9 oz) lobster
Salt and pepper
1 cup sherry or madeira

Melt the butter in a casserole and brown the garlic in it, removing it afterwards. Add the flour and when it is brown, add the stock. Cut the lobster into pieces, add to the stock and season with salt and pepper. Add the sherry or madeira just before serving. Garnish with croûtons.

Sopa de Sesos
Brain Soup

1 set calves' brains
2 handfuls swiss chard
100 g (4 oz) grated cheese
Salt and pepper to taste
1 egg white

50 g (2 oz) flour
Oil or lard
1 cup tomato purée (p. 18)
1½ litres (3 pints) stock
1 tablespoon chopped parsley

Boil the cleaned brains with salt, and when they go white remove the outer membrane. In another pan boil the swiss chard with a little bicarbonate of soda. Drain, pressing against the side of the sieve to get rid of all the moisture. Grind or blend the brains and swiss chard together.

Add the grated cheese and salt and pepper to taste. Make small balls of this mixture about the size of a hazelnut, dip these into the lightly beaten white of egg, then coat with flour. Brown in very hot oil or lard. Add the tomato purée to the boiling stock and add a little of the chopped parsley and a little pepper. Place the balls in the soup tureen and pour over the piping hot stock, serving immediately.

Caldo de Tocino y Frijol
Bean and Bacon Soup

150 g (5½ oz) bacon
1 raw ham bone
250 g (9 oz) haricot beans

500 g (1 lb 2 oz) medium
  potatoes
2 tablespoons maize flour
3 cabbage leaves

Boil the bacon, the ham bone and the beans (soaked overnight) in 4 litres (7 pints) of water, adding more as required, for 3 hours. Remove the bone and add the peeled, diced potatoes and the flour. Boil for 15 minutes, then add the finely shredded cabbage. Boil for a further 15 minutes and serve piping hot. Almost a meal in itself.

Potaje de Frijol Blanco o de Garbanzo
Haricot Bean or Chick-pea Soup

500 g (1 lb 2 oz) haricot beans
  or chick-peas
½ medium-sized onion
2 tablespoons oil
50 g (2 oz) raw ham
2 chorizos (see p. 17)
1 bay leaf

1 sprig thyme
2 large tomatoes
Salt and pepper to taste
½ teaspoon oregano
2 tortillas
Grated cheese

Soak the beans or chick-peas overnight in salted water. The following day boil the beans (approximately 2 hours) or the chick-peas (2–6 hours depending on the quality of the pulse) in fresh water until they are done. This process is speeded by pressure cooking. Fry the sliced onion in the oil and when it is golden brown add the chopped ham and sliced chorizo. Stir in the bay leaf and thyme and immediately add the tomatoes, previously lightly boiled, skinned and sieved to remove the seeds. Add a little salt and pepper and add to the pot with the beans or chick-peas which should be allowed to boil a little longer, taking care that they do not disintegrate.

The soup may be garnished with oregano; the tortillas cut into squares and fried, and with some grated cheese.

Sopa de Elote Molido
Sweet Corn Soup

6 *corns on the cob or 2 tins*
  sweet corn
1 *onion*
50 *g (2 oz) butter*
6 *tablespoons tomato purée*
(*p.* 18)

2 *litres (3½ pints) chicken*
  stock
Salt and pepper
½ *cup cream*

Boil the cobs till tender and scrape the kernels from them. If tinned sweet corn is used, strain off the juice. Grind up the corn kernels in an electric blender or by passing them through a sieve once tender.

Chop the onion and fry in butter till golden brown. Add the tomato purée, the ground corn, the stock, salt and pepper and leave to simmer till the soup has thickened. Remove from the heat and when slightly cooled add the cream and serve immediately.

Half a pint of milk may be substituted for the cream if 1 tablespoon of flour is added to the onion. The milk is added whilst stirring vigorously and the sauce allowed to thicken before the addition of the tomato purée.

Sopa de Aguacate
Avocado Soup

This soup works out rather expensive because of the exorbitant price of avocados in Britain but the subtly flavoured creamy velouté which results is well worth every penny.

4 *tablespoons butter*	5 *large avocados*
2 *tablespoons flour*	½ *cup cream*
½ *teaspoon onion juice*	2 *tortillas*
2 *litres (3½ pints) stock*	2 *tablespoons lard*
Salt and pepper	

Melt the butter in a deep casserole and stir in the flour. Before it browns, add the onion juice, the meat stock and the salt and pepper and leave to simmer till fairly thick. Remove from the heat. Mash the avocados and mix with the cream, using an electric blender if available. Cut the tortillas into small squares and fry in hot lard. Pour the hot soup over the avocado and cream mixture. Garnish with the tortilla croûtons and serve immediately.

Sopa de Calabaza
Courgette Soup

250 g (9 oz) *tender marrow or courgette peelings*	2 *tablespoons flour*
	2 *egg yolks*
2 *litres (3½ pints) meat stock*	50 g (2 oz) *salted crackers*
1 *onion*	½ *cup cream*
50 g (2 oz) *butter*	

Boil the courgette or marrow peelings in 1 litre (1¾ pints) of the stock with the onion and salt to taste. When the peelings are tender, mash or blend, dissolving them in their stock. Strain and mix with the rest of the stock. Melt the butter in a deep casserole and stir in the flour. Before it browns, add the courgette-flavoured stock. Adjust seasoning and simmer till thickened. Remove from the heat. When it has cooled a little, add the well-beaten egg yolks and the crackers crumbled and mixed with the cream. Serve immediately.

Sopa de Espinaca
Spinach Soup

3 tablespoons butter
1 tablespoon flour
1½ litres (3 pints) milk
1 cup cooked, chopped
  spinach

2 red peppers
Salt and pepper to taste
Pinch of ground nutmeg

Melt the butter in a deep casserole. Stir in the flour and add
the milk, stirring constantly so that no lumps form, until it
comes to the boil. Add the chopped spinach and the chopped
red peppers. Season with salt and pepper. Serve very hot
sprinkled with nutmeg and garnished with crumbled
crackers and grated cheese.

Sopa de Chicharos
Pea Soup

More than a soup, this would serve as a light meal on its
own.

2 cups peas
1½ litres (3 pints) stock
2 medium-sized onions
1 egg

Nutmeg and salt to taste
1 tablespoon chopped parsley
½ tablespoon butter

Boil the peas in a little stock with the quartered onions. Mix
(do not beat) the egg with a little salt, nutmeg, the parsley
and the butter. Leave for half an hour. Take up small
teaspoonfuls of the egg mixture and add to the boiling soup.
If balls do not form, add a little flour to the egg mixture.
Season the soup to taste and serve immediately.

Sopa de Poro y Papa
Leek and Potato Soup

2 *large leeks*
2 *large potatoes*
2 *tablespoons butter*

2 *litres (3½ pints) basic stock*
   (p. 28) or water
Salt and pepper to taste

Slice the leeks finely and peel and chop the potatoes in fine strips. Melt the butter in a frying-pan and lightly brown the leeks. Fry some pieces of potato in the same pan. Put all the potatoes and leeks to boil in the warm stock or water. Season with salt and plenty of pepper. Boil so that the potatoes disintegrate a little and thicken the soup.

Sopa de Tallarines Verdes
Green Pasta Soup

4 *lettuce leaves*
6 *spinach leaves*
1 *sprig parsley*
1 *small onion*
1 *clove garlic*
1 *egg*

1 *large tablespoon oil*
1 *tablespoon butter*
250 g (9 oz) *flour*
1½ *litres (3 pints) stock*
½ *cup tomato purée (p. 18)*
Salt to taste

The lettuce and spinach leaves, parsley, onion and garlic are ground finely and mixed with the egg, the oil and melted butter and finally with the flour. When well mixed, roll out on a table, forming a large tortilla about the thickness of a 50p piece, making sure that it is the same thickness all over. Cut strips about 1 cm (¼-½ in) wide, the whole length of the tortilla. Place on a clean napkin and leave to air until the following day.

Fry the pasta in plenty of lard and add to the meat stock with the tomato purée. Allow to simmer for a few minutes, then serve.

Sopa de Lechuga
Mexican Lettuce Soup

12 *large lettuce leaves*
3 *tablespoons oil*
4 *eggs*
Salt and pepper
1 *small onion*

2 *cloves garlic*
2 *tomatoes*
1 *litre (1¾ pints) chicken
stock*

Wash the lettuce leaves. (These may be left-over leaves but remove any brownish pieces.) Dry and chop into small pieces. Heat the oil in a heavy-bottomed (omelette) pan. Beat the eggs with the salt and pepper and add the lettuce, mixing well. Make an egg and lettuce omelette, covering the pan. Lower the heat and when the bottom of the omelette has browned, turn it over and cook the underside till browned.

Meanwhile, chop the onion and garlic and fry together in a little oil till brown. Then add the tomatoes, chopped fine. Leave to reduce. The sauce can be mashed with a potato-masher or put through a mouli grinder to give added smoothness. Add the sauce to the boiling stock. Finally, cut the lettuce omelette into small cubes and add to the boiling soup. Leave to simmer for 15 to 30 minutes. Serve piping hot, garnished with grated cheese.

Dry Soups (Pasta)

'Dry' soups are made with a good stock in which rice or pasta, such as spaghetti, macaroni or noodles, or alternatively tortillas are cooked, generally with tomatoes, onions, garlic and herbs. The stock is all absorbed, imparting its flavour to the rice. Mexicans generally have a dry soup before launching into their meat course. The quantities given for the recipes in this section are sufficient as a starter. Some of the recipes, however, are nutritious enough to make a complete meal in themselves but you will have to double the quantities for six persons.

Arroz Blanco a la Mexicana
Mexican White Rice

Highly recommended, this is the most popular 'dry' soup, eaten almost every day before the meat course. It should be served on a separate plate with lashings of *salsa roja* and is often topped with a fried egg.

200 g (7 oz) long-grain white rice	4 tablespoons tomato purée (p. 18)
1 small onion	1 clove garlic
4 tablespoons lard	½ litre (1 pint) stock
2 large tomatoes	Salt
	1 tablespoon chopped parsley

Soak the rice in hot water for 30 minutes. Strain and wash it well in cold water. Drain well. Fry the onion in the lard in a large flat-bottomed, preferably earthenware, casserole with a lid until golden brown. Fry the rice in the same fat until it becomes transparent and lightly browned. Drain off any excess fat.

Add the fried onion, the tomatoes, the tomato purée and

the crushed garlic to the fried rice and leave to simmer until dry, stirring occasionally. Add the boiling stock, salted to taste, stir well and turn the heat down to a very low light. Put the lid firmly on the casserole so that none of the liquid can escape and leave to cook for 25 minutes WITHOUT STIRRING. Test the rice on the top – when pinched between the fingers, there should be no hard white part in the centre and each grain should be separate. A little more water may be sprinkled over the rice if it has absorbed all the liquid without being cooked but on no account should it be vigorously stirred as the grains will then not remain separate. When ready, the rice should be put on one side with the lid on to rest for about 5 minutes before serving, garnished with the chopped parsley.

If desired a few peas can be added to the rice with the onion and tomatoes. To make a more complete meal, garnish the rice with slices of fried chorizo (see p. 17), hard-boiled egg and avocado.

Arroz Verde
Green Rice

250 g (9 oz) long-grain white rice	100 g (4 oz) lard
	½ litre (1 pint) meat stock
6 large poblano chiles or 3 medium green peppers	50 g (2 oz) butter
	50 g (2 oz) grated cheese
1 onion	Salt
1 clove garlic	

Soak the rice in hot water for 30 minutes. Rinse in cold water and drain well. Toast and de-vein the chiles or green peppers (if fresh) and grind them together with the onion and garlic. Fry the rice in the lard in a heavy-bottomed casserole with a lid. Pour off the fat and add the ground chile, onion and garlic. Add the meat stock and salt to taste. Cover the pot and leave to simmer on a very low light until the rice dries out (about 25 minutes). Dot with butter and continue cooking until the rice is dry and separate. Remove from the heat and leave to rest for 15 minutes before serving, garnished with the grated cheese.

Arroz con Pollo
Rice and Chicken

Double the quantities for a main meal for six.

250 g (9 oz) long-grain white
  rice
500 g (1 lb 2 oz) chicken
1 small onion
1 clove garlic
6 tablespoons oil
2 large green peppers

1 tablespoon chopped parsley
1 bay leaf
100 g (4 oz) peas
12 saffron needles (or
  1 teaspoon turmeric)
Salt to taste

Soak the rice for 30 minutes in hot water. Rinse thoroughly and drain well. Cut the chicken in small pieces. Chop and fry the onion and garlic and when they begin to brown, add the chicken and then one of the peppers cut in rings. When these have browned, drain off the oil and reserve. Add 1 litre (1¾ pints) of water, the parsley and bay leaf and salt. Leave to boil for 30 minutes until the chicken is cooked. Then add the peas and the saffron which should be toasted a little and dissolved in water or a tablespoon of vinegar. Leave to cook for a further 15 minutes and when everything is done, add the rice, previously fried in the oil used for the onion, garlic and chicken. Adjust the amount of stock in the casserole so that there is the right amount for the rice to absorb (½ litre/1 pint). Leave to simmer on a very low heat with a close-fitting lid for 25 minutes. Remove from the heat and leave to rest for 15 minutes before serving. Garnish each plate with strips of the remaining green pepper which should be toasted and peeled. If the saffron does not give enough colour, add some turmeric or paprika.

Arroz con Puerco
Pork and Rice

For a complete meal for six, double all quantities and use 500 g (1 lb 2 oz) pork loin.

250 g (9 oz) long-grain white
  rice
100 g (4 oz) pork loin
3 tablespoons oil
1 clove garlic
½ small onion
1 large tomato

100 g (4 oz) potatoes
100 g (4 oz) peas
1 tablespoon chopped parsley
1 poblano chile or small green
  pepper
Salt to taste

Soak the rice in hot water for 30 minutes. Rinse well and drain thoroughly. Cut the pork into small pieces and brown in the oil. Add the rice and when it is transparent and lightly browned, add the crushed garlic, chopped onion and tomatoes, the diced raw potatoes and the peas. Leave to simmer for 5 or 10 minutes, then add ½ litre (1 pint) of water, the parsley and salt and the whole poblano chile. Leave on a very low light in a casserole with a heavy lid without stirring for 25 minutes or until the water has been absorbed. Leave to rest off the heat for 15 minutes before serving.

Arroz con Jamon
Rice with Ham

Double the quantities for a main meal for six.

200 g (7 oz) long-grain white
  rice
100 g (4 oz) ham
1 red pepper
1 tablespoon chopped parsley
1 tablespoon chopped onion

12 chopped olives
3 eggs
50 g (2 oz) butter
100 g (4 oz) grated cheese
½ cup breadcrumbs
Salt and pepper

Make some Mexican white rice (see p. 38) or simply boil the
rice or use left-overs from yesterday. Butter a heat-proof
dish. Put the cooked rice on the bottom and up the sides of
the dish. Chop the ham and mix with the chopped pepper,
the parsley, onion and olives. Add the well-beaten eggs and
season with salt and pepper. Place the mixture in the centre
of the rice. Scatter with breadcrumbs, grated cheese and
dots of butter and put in a moderate oven until the egg has
set.

Budin de Arroz con Espinacas
Rice and Spinach Pie

A good way of using up left-over rice.

4 *cups Mexican white rice* (*see p.* 38)	1 *cup cooked, chopped spinach*
2 *cups cheese sauce*	

Mix the rice with the finely chopped spinach. Butter a
baking dish and fill it with the mixture, pressing it down
firmly. Cook in a *bain marie* for 30 minutes. Meanwhile
make a cheese sauce. Turn out the rice and spinach mould
on a warmed plate and serve with the cheese sauce poured
over it.

Frituras de Arroz
Rice Rissoles

Another delicious way of using up left-over rice.

1½ *cups left-over white rice*	3 *tablespoons lard*
½ *cup chopped cooked ham*	2 *firm tomatoes*
1 *tablespoon finely chopped onion*	1 *small handful parsley*
3 *eggs*	*Salt and pepper to taste*

Mix well the rice, chopped ham, onion, salt and pepper. Add the beaten egg-yolks and then the whites, beaten until they form peaks. Fry spoonfuls of the rice mixture in really hot fat and serve immediately garnished with the chopped parsley and quartered tomatoes.

Although rice is by far the most popular 'dry soup', the changes can be rung with macaroni, spaghetti, ravioli and tortillas.

Macarron a la Mexicana
Mexican Macaroni

200 g (7 oz) macaroni	6 peppercorns
Salt	½ cup grated cheese
1 onion	6 tablespoons butter

Sauce

4 large poblano chiles or small green peppers	1 cup cream
	Salt and pepper

Boil the macaroni in 2 litres (3½ pints) of water with 1 tablespoon of salt, the quartered onion and the peppercorns. When tender (after 14 minutes in rapidly boiling water), rinse in cold water and drain.

To make the sauce: Toast the chiles and leave them to sweat in a damp cloth. Remove the skin and de-vein them. Grind them up with the cream and add salt and pepper.

Butter a baking dish and put in layers of macaroni, grated cheese, sauce and dots of butter until the dish is filled. Brown lightly in the oven or under a moderate grill and serve immediately.

A variation on this is to chop up some ham and substitute it for the chile in the layers.

Macarrones con Jamon
Macaroni with Ham

Use double quantities for a main meal for six.

200 g (7 oz) macaroni	Salt and pepper
200 g (7 oz) ham	200 g (7 oz) butter
1 tablespoon lard	100 g (4 oz) Gruyère cheese
500 g (1 lb 2 oz) tomatoes	100 g (4 oz) Edam cheese

The macaroni is cooked in plenty of boiling, salted water until tender (14 minutes). Drain and wash thoroughly in cold water. Drain well. Fry the chopped ham in 1 tablespoon lard. Remove and fry the skinned, sieved tomatoes with some salt and pepper in the same fat. Put a little butter or oil in the bottom of a casserole and heat gently. Remove from the heat and place in layers the macaroni, the tomatoes, the grated cheese, pieces of ham and small knobs of butter, ending with a layer of cheese and butter. Brown for 20 minutes in a moderate oven and serve immediately.

Croquetas de Macarron
Macaroni Croquettes

100 g (4 oz) macaroni	2 eggs
1 green pepper	1 cup breadcrumbs
3 chopped hard-boiled eggs	Lard or oil for frying
¼ litre (½ pint) thick white sauce	

Boil the macaroni in plenty of boiling, salted water for 14 minutes. Drain and run cold water over it. Cut in small pieces. Chop the green pepper and fry for a few minutes. Mix with the macaroni, chopped hard-boiled egg and the thick white sauce. Season with salt and pepper and leave to cool.

Take large spoonfuls of the mixture and form macaroni balls with the hands. Dip each in the beaten egg and then the breadcrumbs and fry in good hot lard or oil. A little cheese may be added to the macaroni mixture if desired. Serve on their own or with a tomato sauce.

Spaghetti Blanco a la Mexicana
Mexican White Spaghetti

Double the quantities for a main dish for six persons.

200 g (7 oz) spaghetti	100 g (4 oz) Parmesan cheese
150 g (5 oz) butter	100 g (4 oz) Edam cheese
¼ litre (½ pint) cream	100 g (4 oz) ham
2 tablespoons chopped parsley	Salt and pepper
1 tablespoon very finely chopped onion	

Boil the spaghetti in lightly salted water for 14 minutes. Drain and wash well with cold water. Drain well. Put a tablespoon of melted butter or oil in a casserole. Put in a layer of spaghetti, then one of the cream in which you have stirred the parsley and onion. If the cream is very thick a little milk should be added but the total should not be more than ¼ litre (½ pint). Then put a layer of the grated Parmesan, the Edam in strips, the ham cut in small squares, pieces of butter and pepper and salt. Repeat the layers, ending with cheese and butter and a little cream. Brown slightly in a moderate oven (half an hour).

Raviolis Mexicanos
Mexican Ravioli

Double the quantities for a main meal for six.

250 g (9 oz) tortilla dough
1 teaspoon baking powder
100 g (4 oz) flour
1 egg and 1 white

200 g (7 oz) lard
100 g (4 oz) grated cheese
50 g (2 oz) butter

For the sauce
1 onion
3 poblano chiles or small
  green peppers

1 cup tomato purée (p. 18)
Salt and pepper to taste

Knead the tortilla dough together with the baking powder,
flour, the beaten egg and 1 tablespoon of soft lard. Roll out
to ½ cm (⅛ in) in thickness and cut into small rounds. Put a
little grated cheese in the centre of each round and fold over.
Seal the edges with egg white and fry in good hot lard. In a
well-greased baking-dish place layers of ravioli, sauce,
grated cheese and dots of butter. Bake in a moderate oven
for half an hour and serve.

To make the sauce: Brown the finely chopped onion with
the toasted, de-veined, sliced chiles or peppers, the tomato
purée, salt and pepper. Simmer till thickened.

Tallarines con Chorizo
Pasta (Macaroni, Spaghetti or Noodles) with Chorizo

Double the quantities for a main meal for six.

250 g (9 oz) pasta
1 small onion
6 peppercorns
2 bay leaves
1 sprig thyme
2 chorizos (see p. 17)

lard
1½ cups tomato purée (p. 18)
Chopped parsley
Salt and pepper
100 g (4 oz) grated cheese
50 g (2 oz) butter

Cook the pasta in plenty of boiling, salted water with half
the onion, the peppercorns, bay leaves and thyme. When
tender, rinse in cold water and drain well.

Fry the chorizo in lard and in the same fat sauté the other half onion and the tomato purée. Add a little chopped parsley. Season with salt and pepper and leave to thicken. Grease a baking dish and arrange in it layers of noodles, sauce, grated cheese, fried chorizo and dots of butter. Brown in a moderate oven or under a low grill for 30 minutes and serve.

Pastel de Pobre
Poor Man's Cake

A delicious layered dish using left-over tortillas, the result resembling lasagna.

200 g (7 oz) tortillas
4 tablespoons lard
1 onion
4 poblano chiles or small
   green peppers
1 cup tomato purée (p. 18)

1 clove garlic
Salt and pepper
1 cup cream
50 g (2 oz) grated cheese
150 g (5 oz) butter

Trim off the edges of the tortillas and cut into macaroni-sized strips. Fry lightly in the lard but do not brown.

Make the sauce: Chop the onion and sauté in lard with the toasted, skinned and de-veined chiles, the tomato purée, the crushed garlic and salt and pepper. Leave to simmer until thick.

Arrange alternate layers of fried tortilla, sauce, cream, grated cheese and dots of butter. Brown in a moderate oven for 30 minutes and serve.

Fish

With miles of coastline, both on the Pacific and on the Caribbean, Mexicans can enjoy a wide variety of sea-food. Whilst the states on the East coast, Veracruz, Tamaulipas, Campeche and Tabasco, have special ways of cooking *huachinango* (red snapper), octopus and turtle, on the West coast the speciality in Acapulco is *ceviche* (p. 23), shrimps in Nayarit, oysters in Sinaloa and *caguama*, a species of sea-turtle, in Baja California.

Recipes in this section suggest suitable alternatives for types of fish which are not available in Britain.

Ostiones en Escabeche
Pickled Oysters

A dish from the state of Sinaloa, which indicates the vast extent of its coastline.

24 *fresh oysters in their shells*
2 *teaspoons lemon juice*
½ *teaspoon salt*
½ *cup olive oil*
2 *cloves garlic*
2 *peppercorns*
4 *tablespoons vinegar*
½ *tin jalapeño chiles*
2 *kg* (4½ *lb*) *crushed ice,*
   coloured green

Steam open the oysters in a well-covered pot. Remove the oysters from their shells and place in a pan containing 4 tablespoons of water and 2 teaspoons of lemon juice and ½ teaspoon salt. Boil for 2 minutes. Drain well and fry the oysters lightly in the oil.

Toast the garlic and peppercorns, grind and add to the vinegar. Add the oysters, their juice and the chiles, cut into strips. Cover the dish and set aside for 3 hours.

Serve the oysters in their shells, arranging them on a tray placed over the green-tinted crushed ice.

Camarones en Frío
Pickled Shrimps

This is a favourite dish in Nayarit in the north-west of Mexico.

1 kg (2¼ lb) fresh shrimps	3 cloves garlic
¼ litre (½ pint) oil	3 large tomatoes
4 large onions	

Sauce

⅛ litre (¼ pint) vinegar	Dry mustard, salt and pepper
1 tin jalapeño chiles	

Clean and rinse the fresh shrimps. Slice one of the onions and the garlic and fry in the hot oil. Remove. Fry the shrimps in the same oil until they go soft. Remove from the fat and set on absorbent paper to cool. Chill.

To make the sauce: Add the vinegar to half the oil. Season to taste with mustard, the juice from the tin of chiles, salt and pepper. Pour the sauce over the chilled shrimps. Garnish with slices of the remaining onions, previously soaked for 2 hours in lemon juice, slices of tomato and strips of jalapeño chile.

Tortitas de Bacalao
Cod Fritters

250 g (9 oz) salt cod	1 lettuce
1 tablespoon chopped parsley	1 lemon
1 small onion	Oil for frying

Batter

100 g (4 oz) flour	¼ litre (½ pint) tepid water
3 tablespoons olive oil	White of 1 egg
Pinch salt	

Cut the salt cod into bite-sized pieces and leave to soak overnight. The following day, rinse thoroughly and boil in fresh water. When cooked, mix with the finely chopped onion and parsley.

Mix the flour with the olive oil, add the salt and water and stir to a smooth cream. Leave to stand for 2 hours. Stir in the stiffly beaten egg white.

Dip the pieces of fish into the batter and fry till golden brown in very hot fat. Serve with a dressed salad and wedges of lemon.

Bacalao a la Mexicana
Cod Mexican Style

1 *medium-sized onion*	2 *tablespoons chopped parsley*
2 *cloves garlic*	4 *tablespoons oil*
1 *green pepper*	500 *g* (1 *lb* 2 *oz*) *potatoes*
500 *g* (1 *lb* 2 *oz*) *tomatoes*	*Pepper, bay leaf and thyme*
500 *g* (1 *lb* 2 *oz*) *salt cod*	24 *olives*

Cut the cod into small pieces and soak overnight. Next day, throw away the water and rinse well. Cook in fresh water and remove when it is done. Chop and brown the onion and garlic, adding the sliced green pepper and finally the finely chopped parsley and tomatoes. Add the fish, cooked and diced potatoes, pepper and herbs to taste. Add a little of the fish stock. Leave simmering to season for a few minutes and serve garnished with the olives.

Pescado o Bacalao en Mojo Rojo
Cod or White Fish in a Fiery Sauce

1½ *kg (3½ lb) fresh white fish*   1 *kg (2¼ lb) potatoes*
    or 500 *g (1 lb 2 oz) salt cod*   1 *medium-sized onion*

Mojo (Sauce)
15 *cloves garlic*   50 *g (2 oz) paprika*
5 *tablespoons oil*

If using cod, cut into small pieces and soak overnight. Next day, throw away the water and cook in fresh water with the quartered onion. When the cod is tender, add the quartered potatoes and when these are cooked remove the fish and potatoes from the stock and serve with the *Mojo (sauce)*.

If using fresh fish, cut in thick portions early in the day and sprinkle with salt. Boil the potatoes with the onion and when these are tender, add the fish. When cooked, drain off the stock and serve, covered in the sauce.

For the Mojo: Fry the cloves of garlic in oil till dark brown but not burnt. Remove from the heat to cool. Add the paprika and put on the heat for a moment, stirring so that the paprika does not burn. Add 2 tablespoons of the fish stock. Pour over the fish and serve.

Bacalao o Pescado en Mojo Verde
Cod or White Fish in Green Sauce

1½ *kilos (3½ lb) fresh white*   1 *kilo (2¼ lb) potatoes*
    fish or ½ *kilo (1 lb 2 oz) salt*   1 *medium-sized onion*
    cod

Mojo Verde (Green Sauce)

5 tablespoons chopped parsley   5 tablespoons oil
5 cloves garlic

Prepare the fish as in the previous recipe, this time pouring over it the green sauce instead of the red one.

To make the Mojo Verde (Green Sauce): Grind the parsley and moisten with a little of the water in which the fish was cooked. Fry the cloves of garlic in the oil and then add the parsley. Pour the hot sauce over the fish and serve.

Adobo de Pescado
Fish in Adobo Sauce

A recipe from the state of Tamaulipas, which stretches north to the United States border and east to the Gulf of Mexico.

6 slices red snapper or	*1 lettuce*
haddock	*1 bunch radishes*
½ cup oil	*Vinegar, salt and pepper*

Sauce

4 ancho chiles	*1 teaspoon oregano*
2 onions	*500 g (1 lb 2 oz) tomatoes*
3 cloves garlic	*Juice of 2 oranges*
4 cumin seeds	

Sprinkle salt over the slices of fish, fry them lightly in the oil and remove.

For the sauce: Toast the chiles, clean and grind with the onion, garlic, cumin seeds, oregano and tomato. Sauté these ingredients in the oil used for the fish. Remove from the heat and add the orange juice.

Butter a casserole and arrange the slices of fish in layers, pouring sauce over each layer. Put a lid on the casserole and cook in a moderate oven for 30 minutes. Serve the fish with a salad made with finely shredded lettuce, pieces of radish, oil, vinegar, salt and pepper.

Pescado a la Veracruzana
Fish Veracruz Style

1 kg (2¼ lb) sliced red snapper
   or filleted haddock
Salt and pepper
1 lemon
6 tablespoons oil
2 cloves garlic
3 onions

700 g (1½ lb) tomatoes,
   puréed
2 cups fish stock
75 g (3 oz) olives
50 g (2 oz) capers
6 pickled jalapeño chiles
   (see p. 127)

Rub the slices of fish with salt, pepper and lemon juice. Fry the cloves of garlic in the oil and remove. In the same oil, lightly brown the sliced onions. Add the tomato purée, the fish stock (made by boiling up the fish heads), salt and pepper, the fish, olives, capers and chiles. Leave to simmer on a low heat until the fish is done and the sauce is thick.

Pescado en Salsa de Almendras
Fish in Almond Sauce

1 kg (2¼ lb) haddock
Salt and pepper
6 tablespoons oil
100 g (4 oz) almonds

3 hard-boiled eggs
2 tablespoons mustard
1 tablespoon chopped parsley
3 lemons

Sprinkle the fresh haddock fillets with salt, pepper and 3 tablespoons of oil. Place on a greased baking-tray in a moderate oven for 30 minutes.

Soak the almonds overnight in cold water, peel and grind. Mix with the egg yolks (broken with a fork), the mustard,

3 tablespoons of oil and the parsley. Season with salt and pepper, adding the chopped egg white.

Pour the sauce over the fish and serve, garnished with pieces of lemon.

Pescado a la Poblana
Fish Pueblan Style

1½ *kilos* (3½ *lb*) *haddock*	500 *g* (1 *lb* 2 *oz*) *cooked peas*
2 *lemons*	*Mayonnaise* (*see p*. 131)
4 *tablespoons oil*	100 *g* (4 *oz*) *butter*
Salt and pepper to taste	12 *spring onions*

Rub the fish fillets with lemon, oil, salt and pepper and place on a greased baking-tray. Put in a hot oven for 30 minutes. Put the fish on a warmed plate and surround it with the drained peas. Cover with thick mayonnaise and garnish with dots of butter, thin slices of lemon and spring onions. Serve immediately.

Pescado a la Jarocha
Fish Jarochan Style

6 *haddock fillets*	3 *tablespoons fresh double*
Salt and pepper	*cream*
1 *lemon*	1 *tablespoon chopped parsley*
1 *tablespoon oil*	24 *olives*
Mayonnaise (*see p*. 131)	

Sprinkle the fish fillets with salt, pepper, lemon juice and a tablespoon of oil. Place on a greased baking-tray and cook in a fairly hot oven for 30 minutes. Mix the mayonnaise with the cream, parsley and chopped, stoned olives. Pour over the fish and serve immediately.

Filetes de Pescado al Horno
Fish Fillets in the Oven

6 *large haddock fillets*
1 *large red pepper*
6 *rashers bacon*
Salt and pepper to taste
1 *onion*

1 *bay leaf*
1 *cup white wine*
2 *lemons*
Cress

Take a fillet of fish and place a strip of red pepper across the middle of it so that it sticks out at each side (if one will not stretch, use two). Roll up the fillet. Cut the bacon rashers down the middle and wrap a piece round each end of the rolled-up fish fillet, securing with toothpicks.

Sprinkle each fillet with salt and pepper. Place on a well-greased baking-tray and put in a hot oven. When the bacon is golden brown and the grease has come out of it, add the bay leaf and the onion cut in rings. After a few more minutes, add the white wine. Serve very hot, garnished with pieces of lemon and cress.

Pulpos en su Tinta
Octopus in its Ink

1 *kg* (2¼ *lb*) *octopus*
2 *bay leaves*
6 *cumin seeds*
4 *peppercorns*
4 *tablespoons olive oil*

1 *medium-sized onion*
4 *cloves garlic*
1 *kg* (2¼ *lb*) *tomatoes*
100 *g* (4 *oz*) *sweet chiles*
1 *tablespoon chopped parsley*

Remove the ink, internal organs, eyes and beak from the octopus and wash well in salt water, reserving the ink. The larger octopi should be beaten. Rinse and cut into small pieces. Grind the bay leaves and spices. Fry the chopped onions and garlic and then the tomatoes, chopped, sweet chiles and parsley. When this comes to the boil, add the octopus meat. Cover and leave to cook for 30 minutes. Add the spices and the ink and continue cooking until all the liquids have been boiled off and the octopus is left in the oil only (2–2½ hours on a low heat).

Caldo Miche
Jaliscan Fish Stew

700 g (1½ lb) tomatoes
8 small green chiles
3 onions
2 bay leaves
3 cloves garlic

Oregano and coriander leaf
   to taste
1 kg (2¼ lb) catfish
3 greengages

Chop the tomatoes, chiles (reserving a few for garnish) and onions and place to boil in 2 litres (4 pints) of water with the herbs and some salt. When the onion is tender, add the fish. Leave to cook for 5 minutes, then remove and skin. Put the fish back in the broth and cook 5 minutes longer until evenly seasoned. Add the sliced greengages. Do not stir too much or the fish will disintegrate. Serve as soon as the fish is done (after about 20 minutes).

Timbales de Pescado
Fish Moulds

250 g (9 oz) cooked fish or
   tinned salmon or tuna
1 cup breadcrumbs
1 egg
½ cup milk or cream

2 tablespoons lemon juice
Salt and pepper
2 cups white sauce
1 cup cooked peas
2 tablespoons chopped parsley

Mix the fish and the breadcrumbs with the beaten egg, lemon juice, cream, salt and pepper. Butter 6 individual moulds, fill with the mixture and cook in a *bain marie* with very little water till they are firm enough to turn out without disintegrating (30 minutes). Turn out on to a warm plate and serve with the white sauce and peas, garnished with chopped parsley.

Poultry

TURKEY

Turkey has always been a Christmas dish in Britain but has now become very good value pound for pound and is available all year round. Most country people in Mexico keep a few *guajalotes* and other poultry in their back yard, and even in Mexico City one is awoken by cocks crowing. Here are some recipes you might like to try if you are feeding a multitude.

Mole (pronounced *moll-ay*)

Mole is one of the greatest of the traditional Mexican dishes, having a sumptuous sauce comprised of chile, dark chocolate, nuts and spices. It is also one of the most difficult dishes to reproduce without the correct chiles and the green tomatoes. These are, however, available in tins or dried and a very good approximation can be produced using unripe British tomatoes.

1 *turkey*
1 *cup lard*
10 *ancho chiles*
4 *pasilla chiles*
8 *mulato chiles*
2 *slices bread*
3 *tortillas*
3 *tomatoes*
15 *green tomatoes*
   (tomates, *see p.* 18)
6 *tablespoons pumpkin seeds*
3 *tablespoons chile seeds*
2 *tablespoons sesame seeds*
3 *tablespoons almonds*
3 *tablespoons peanuts*
6 *cloves*
6 *black peppercorns*
1 *stick cinnamon*
3 *cloves garlic*
100 g (4 oz) *chocolate*
1 *tablespoon sugar*

Cut the turkey into smallish pieces and put on to boil with some salt in enough water to cover.

Remove the veins from the chiles and fry lightly. Fry together the bread, tortillas, tomatoes, green tomatoes, pumpkin seeds, chile seeds, sesame seeds, almonds and peanuts. When they have browned, cool slightly, then grind or pulverise. Add the cloves, pepper, cinnamon and garlic, which should be ground together. Fry the mixture again in very hot fat, stirring well. When it boils, add the chocolate, ground chiles, a tablespoon of sugar and 1 litre (1¾ pints) of turkey stock. When it is thick, add another litre (1¾ pints) of stock and the well-cooked turkey. Continue cooking until the sauce is good and thick. Serve with Mexican white rice (see p. 38), tortillas and beans.

Note: This dish serves 12. A *mole* sauce, using half the ingredients quoted here, can be poured over chicken for more everyday occasions. Any left-over sauce can be kept in concentrated form (simply boil off most of the liquid) in a jar in the fridge for a long time and can be used poured over other meats or as the sauce in *enchiladas* (see p. 107).

Mole Verde
Green Mole

1 *turkey*	100 g (4 oz) *almonds*
2 *onions*	12 *poblano chiles or* 6 *green*
Salt	*peppers*
250 g (9 oz) *pumpkin seeds*	600 g (1 lb 5 oz) *Mexican*
200 g (7 oz) *lard or oil*	*green tomatoes*
100 g (4 oz) *walnuts*	2 *cloves garlic*

Cut the turkey in smallish pieces and place to boil with 1 onion and some salt in plenty of water. Fry the pumpkin seeds in some of the lard or oil and grind. Do the same with the unblanched almonds, the walnuts and the chiles. Peel and grind the tomatoes with one onion and the garlic. Fry in 3 tablespoons of lard. Add the nuts, pumpkin seeds and chiles. Then add 1 litre (2 pints) of the turkey stock and the small pieces of well-cooked turkey. Season with salt and leave to simmer till the sauce has thickened.

Note: This dish serves 12. A green mole sauce, using half the ingredients quoted here, can be poured over chicken for more everyday occasions. Any left-over sauce can be kept in concentrated form (simply boil off most of the liquid) in a jar in the fridge for a long time and can be used poured over other meats or as the sauce in green *enchiladas* (see p. 107).

Pavo con Fruta
Fruity Turkey

This dish serves 12.

1 *turkey*	1 *cup tomato purée* (*p.* 18)
2 *onions*	50 *g* (2 *oz*) *almonds*
Salt and pepper	1 *stick cinnamon*
2 *chorizos* (*see p.* 171)	1 *slice white bread*
4 *tablespoons lard*	150 *g* (5 *oz*) *pineapple*
5 *ancho chiles*	4 *apples*
2 *pasilla chiles* (or 1	2 *bananas*
tablespoon chile powder	10 *pickled chiles* (*see p.* 127)
and ½ *tablespoon flour*)	1 *tablespoon sugar*
3 *cloves garlic*	3 *tablespoons vinegar*

Cut the turkey into small pieces and put on to boil with one onion and salt and pepper in water to cover.

Fry the chorizo in the lard, lift out and in the same fat brown a sliced onion and then add the following ingredients ground together: toasted, cleaned and soaked chiles, garlic, tomato purée, almonds, cinnamon and fried bread. Leave to simmer until thick. Add the pieces of turkey and the stock, the fruit cut in slices, the fried chorizo, the pickled chiles, sugar, vinegar, salt and pepper. Leave to simmer a further 30 minutes until the flavours mingle and the sauce is thick.

Pavo Relleno
Stuffed Turkey

Be daring! Treat your family to an original variation on a familiar theme this Christmas. This dish serves 12.

4½ kg (10 lb) turkey
Salt and pepper
1 lemon
¾ litre (1¼ pints) stock
1 bottle white wine
1 onion
50 g (2 oz) lard or butter to taste

2 bay leaves
2 sprigs thyme
2 sprigs marjoram
2 lettuces
3 large tomatoes
Oil and vinegar dressing

For the stuffing:
100 g (4 oz) bacon
50 g (2 oz) lard
1 large onion
1½ kg (3½ lb) minced loin of pork
⅛ litre (¼ pint) tomato purée (p. 18)

100 g (4 oz) olives
100 g (4 oz) blanched almonds
3 bananas
3 apples
100 g (4 oz) sultanas
1 teaspoon cinnamon
2 teaspoons sugar

For the sauce:
6 jalapeño chiles
1 whole head of garlic
1 large onion
3 carrots

Bay leaf and thyme
Salt and pepper
⅛ litre (¼ pint) vinegar

Rub the turkey inside and out with salt, pepper and lemon juice.

To make the stuffing: Dice and fry the bacon. Remove from the fat and fry the chopped onion in the bacon fat, adding the lard. Add the minced loin of pork, the tomato purée, chopped stoned olives, chopped almonds, diced bananas, apples and sultanas. Season with salt, pepper, cinnamon and sugar. Leave to simmer until thick.

Stuff the turkey with the mixture and brown the bird in the bacon grease. Place in a hot oven in a deep casserole. After half an hour, pour over the meat stock and wine and cover with sliced onion and herbs. Lower the heat of the oven to moderate and leave to roast for a further 3 hours, basting frequently. Put the turkey on a serving dish, straining the gravy and serving it separately. Garnish with sliced tomatoes and shredded lettuce with an oil and vinegar dressing.

To make the chile sauce which accompanies the dish: Devein the jalapeño chiles and cut into strips. Fry in oil with the crushed cloves of garlic, sliced onion and sliced carrots. Add bay leaf and thyme, salt, pepper and vinegar and leave to simmer until the chiles and carrots are tender. Serve cold in a separate bowl.

CHICKEN

Chickens are down in price in Britain these days but just do not have the flavour the free-range ones used to have. Ring the changes with these mouth-watering Mexican recipes, guaranteed to transform even the dullest broiler chick into a meal fit for a king.

Pollo Almendrado
Chicken with Almonds

1 *large tender chicken*	100 g (4 oz) *Mexican green*
1 *onion*	*tomatoes (see p. 18)*
1 *sprig herbs*	1 *cup peas*
Oil for frying	50 g (2 oz) *almonds*
2 *serrano chiles*	*Salt and pepper to taste*

Cut the chicken into pieces and put it to boil in lightly salted water with the halved onion and the herbs. When it comes to the boil, remove the pieces of chicken from the stock and fry in good hot oil for 10 minutes each side. Place the pieces on a sheet of absorbent paper to soak up any excess fat. Fry the green chiles; boil the tomatoes and peas. Fry the almonds with their skins and grind up the chiles, tomatoes, peas and almonds together. Add the chicken stock, salt and pepper and leave to boil. When the sauce thickens, put in the pieces of chicken. Leave for a few minutes so that the flavours mingle. Serve piping hot.

Pollo con Fruta
Fruity Chicken

A sumptuous sweet-and-sour chicken casserole with a hint of the tropics.

1 *large tender chicken*	3 *pears*
2 *cloves garlic*	2 *apples*
1 *small onion*	1 *large banana or plantain*
Salt	2 *strips of pineapple*
250 g (9 oz) *peas*	500 g (1 lb 2 oz) *tomatoes*
250 g (9 oz) *string beans*	2 *tablespoons oil*

Cut the chicken into pieces, wash and put in a saucepan to boil with a piece of garlic, the quartered onion and a pinch of salt. Remove from the stock when cooked.

Pod the peas, string the beans and cut into small pieces. Cook and drain well. Wash, peel and core the pears and apples and cut into medium-sized chunks. Peel the banana and take the centre out of the pineapple. Boil all the fruit together and when the pear is soft, everything is cooked.

Fry the tomato and grind with the garlic and onion. Put through a sieve and fry in hot oil. When it begins to dry, add the fruit, vegetables and chicken. Add two cups of the chicken stock, season with salt and leave to thicken a little before serving.

Tapado de Pollo
Steamed Chicken

A deliciously aromatic dish, this, and highly recommended for a special dinner, as it is actually improved by being prepared in advance and then re-heated before the guests arrive.

2 *large tomatoes*	250 g (9 oz) *pork scraps*
1 *large onion*	*with a bone*
2 *cloves garlic*	*Salt*
2 *tablespoons raisins*	1 *stick cinnamon*
20 *olives*	3 *cloves* (*powdered*)
10 *blanched almonds*	1 *cup water*
1 *tender chicken*	

For best results, this dish should be cooked in an earthenware casserole which should be greased with lard. Place layers of sliced tomato, onion rings, crushed garlic, raisins, olives and almonds in the casserole with the raw pieces of chicken and chunks of pork. Sprinkle each layer with salt, pieces of cinnamon and cloves and finish with a layer of tomato. Add the water, cover the pot with a tight-fitting lid and leave to simmer gently until the meat is cooked and there is a well-seasoned stock. Remove the pork bone and serve piping hot with Mexican or plain white rice.

Pollo en Jugo de Naranja
Chicken in Orange Juice

1 *tender chicken*	2 *glasses fresh orange juice*
Salt and pepper	200 g (7 oz) *small new*
100 g (4 oz) *butter*	*potatoes*
¼ *medium-sized onion*	

Cut the chicken in pieces, singe, wash and sprinkle with salt and pepper. Melt the butter in a casserole and lightly brown a round of onion and then the pieces of chicken. Add the orange juice, cover the pan and leave to boil, making sure the orange juice does not dry up before the chicken is cooked. If necessary, add a little more orange juice or stock. In a separate pot, cook the potatoes and when they are done, add them whole to the casserole and leave them to soak up the flavour of the chicken. Add a little zest of orange and garnish each plate with two segments of orange. Serve good and hot.

Pollo en Jitomate
Chicken and Tomato

1 *tender chicken*	1 *stick cinnamon*
Oil as necessary	1 *small onion*
2 *tablespoons flour*	*Salt and pepper*
3 *tomatoes*	*A little chicken stock or*
50 g (2 oz) *seedless raisins*	*water*
2 *cloves*	

Singe the chicken, cut into pieces, wash and dry with a damp cloth. Fry the chicken in oil and, when golden brown, remove from the fat. Brown the flour in the same fat, taking care that it does not burn. Fry the tomato; peel and grind with the raisins, cloves, cinnamon and onion. Sieve and fry, seasoning with a little salt and pepper. When it begins to thicken, remove from the heat, leave to cool a little and add to the browned flour, stirring so that no lumps are formed. Add a little cold stock, beating well so that all the ingredients are thoroughly mixed, put the sauce back on the heat, add the chicken and leave to boil on a low heat. If necessary, more stock can be added until the chicken is well cooked and the sauce is thick.

Serve piping hot with Mexican white rice.

Pollo en Nogada
Chicken in Walnut Sauce

The walnuts give a special texture and flavour to the sauce, mellowing the piquancy of the chiles.

1 *chicken*	3 *black peppercorns*
6 *ancho chiles*	2 *cloves*
15 g ($\frac{1}{2}$ oz) *white bread*	2 *cloves garlic*
50 g (2 oz) *shelled walnuts*	2 *onions*
50 g (2 oz) *shelled peanuts*	3 *cups chicken stock*
2 *tablespoons lard*	*Salt and pepper*
1 *stick cinnamon*	

Cut the chicken into pieces and put on to boil. Toast, devein and soak the chiles.

Fry the bread, walnuts and peanuts in a tablespoon of the lard. Grind them together with the spices, garlic, onions and chiles. Thin the mixture with a little of the stock and fry in the rest of the lard until it comes to the boil. Add the pieces of well-cooked chicken. Season with salt and pepper and leave to simmer until the sauce is thickened. Serve hot with Mexican white rice and/or tortillas.

Pollo Encacahuatado
Chicken with Peanuts

The subtle combination of peanuts with the milder poblano chiles gives this sauce its distinctive subdued but tangy flavour.

1 *tender chicken*
50 g (2 oz) *lard*
1 *litre* (1¾ *pints*) *stock*
3 *poblano chiles or 2 green*
   peppers

1 *small onion*
100 g (4 oz) *peanuts*
250 g (9 oz) *new potatoes*
Salt and pepper to taste

Singe the chicken, divide into pieces, wash well, dry with a damp cloth and fry in very hot fat. When the pieces are golden brown, add the stock to the same casserole and leave to boil until the liquid is reduced by half.

Fry the chiles, leave them to sweat, wrapped in a damp cloth, remove their skins, de-vein them and grind them with the onion and the peanuts. Mix this sauce with a little stock, sieve it, pour it over the chicken, add the potatoes (cut in half if large) and leave to simmer until well cooked. Serve piping hot with Mexican white rice and/or tortillas.

Pollo Borracho
Drunk Chicken

This dish derives its name from the *pulque* which it traditionally contains. *Pulque* is an alcoholic drink made with the juice from the maguey cactus and is especially popular in the centre of Mexico. It is not available in Britain but bitter orange juice serves magnificently as a substitute. This is a good-looking dish with a slight snap to it.

1 *tender chicken, jointed*
5 *tablespoons oil*
2 *cloves garlic*
1 *onion*
125 g (4½ oz) *tomatoes*
1 *chipotle chile in vinegar*
   (*tinned*)

1 *litre* (1¾ *pints*) *bitter orange*
   juice (or *pulque*)
2 *bay leaves*
1 *sprig marjoram*
1 *sprig thyme*
Salt
2 *bunches spring onions*
1 *avocado*

Fry the pieces of chicken in oil. Remove from the pan when golden brown and in the same oil fry the chopped garlic, the onion, cut in rings, the boiled, ground and sieved tomato, the chipotle chile, cut in small pieces, the orange juice and the herbs. Season with salt and add the pieces of fried chicken. Cover the casserole and leave to cook on a low light. When the chicken is almost done, add the washed spring onions (having removed the leaves). Leave to simmer until the sauce thickens and the chicken is well cooked. Serve hot, garnished with pieces of avocado.

Pollo Verde
Green Chicken

A soothing and highly nutritious dish in which peas are ground to form a thick, creamy blanket over the chicken.

1 *large tender chicken*	1 *cup milk*
1 *tablespoon flour*	*Salt and pepper*
50 g (2 oz) butter	1 *pinch nutmeg*
1 *cup chicken stock*	250 g (9 oz) peas

Cut the chicken into sections and boil in lightly salted water to cover. Fry the flour in the melted butter and before it burns, add the cup of chicken stock and the milk, stirring so that no lumps form. Season with salt, pepper and nutmeg. Add the peas, cooked, ground and sieved, and the pieces of chicken. Leave to boil on a low heat till well seasoned. Serve hot with Mexican white rice.

Pollo Encebollado
Chicken in Onion

A good basic Mexican chicken casserole in which the piquancy of the chile brings out the flavours of the onion, garlic and green pepper.

1 *large chicken*
5 *tablespoons oil*
4 *cloves garlic*
2 *onions*
4 *cups chicken stock*

1 *tablespoon oregano*
2 *green peppers*
50 *g (2 oz) olives*
6 *serrano chiles in vinegar*
Salt

Singe the chicken, cut into pieces, wash and dry with a damp cloth. Boil with a piece of onion and garlic in water to cover.

Heat the oil and fry the garlic in it. Remove from the heat, add the sliced onion and when it is golden, brown the pieces of chicken. Add 3 cups of stock, leave to boil on a low heat and when the stock has reduced, add the oregano, the garlic (ground) with the peppers, cut in strips, and another cup of stock. When the chicken is cooked, add the olives, the chiles in vinegar and salt to taste. Serve with Mexican white rice and tortillas.

Pollo a la Crema
Chicken in Cream

Chile and fresh cream team up well together in this luxurious dish.

1 *large chicken*
125 *g (4½ oz) salted crackers*
Salt and pepper to taste
2 *eggs*
Oil for frying

5 *cloves garlic*
5 *poblano chiles*
¼ *litre (½ pint) fresh cream*
5 *rashers bacon*

Singe the chicken, cut in pieces, wash and dry with a damp cloth. Grind the biscuits well, add the salt and pepper and put in a paper bag. Beat the eggs and put the pieces of chicken in the egg one by one. Then put them in the paper bag. Shake and remove the pieces of chicken covered in the crumbs. Put the oil to heat and burn the garlic in it. Remove the garlic and fry the chicken covered in crumbs, piece by piece, turning it so that it is golden brown on both sides.

Fry the chiles, put to sweat wrapped in a damp cloth, peel, de-vein, cut into strips and rinse so that they are not too piquant. In an earthenware casserole, place layers of chicken, cream, chile and well-fried bacon. Place in a moderate oven for half an hour. Serve hot with Mexican white rice and follow with a green salad.

Pollo al Horno
Chicken Cooked in the Oven

A succulent and tasty way of roasting chicken.

1 *large chicken cut in half*	2 *tablespoons olive oil*
2 *tablespoons lemon juice*	2 *cups tomato purée* (p. 18)
2 *tablespoons oregano*	*Salt and pepper*
4 *tablespoons butter*	

Singe the chicken, wash, leave to drain and rub in the lemon juice combined with the salt and oregano both inside and out. Leave to rest for at least an hour. Put the chicken in an earthenware casserole with the skin to the bottom and spread the butter over it. Put in a hot oven for 30 minutes, then turn the chicken over, pour on the oil and season with pepper. Cover the chicken with the tomato purée, lower the heat to moderate and continue cooking for a further 1½ hours, basting it with the fat so that it does not go dry. Serve with Mexican white rice and a green salad with vinaigrette dressing.

Pollo con Zanahorias
Chicken Carrot Casserole

1 *tender chicken*	3 *cloves*
Oil for frying	1 *sprig thyme*
1 *medium-sized onion*	1 *sprig marjoram*
1 *tablespoon flour*	10 *medium-sized carrots*
3 *cups warm water*	2 *large chiles in vinegar*
Salt and pepper	50 g (2 oz) *olives*

Singe the pieces of chicken, wash well and dry with a damp cloth. Fry the pieces in oil, remove, and fry the finely chopped onion in the same pan. When they are golden brown, remove them, add the flour to the same oil and when it is golden brown, add 3 cups of warm water, stirring vigorously so that no lumps form. When well mixed, add the salt, pepper, cloves, herbs and finally the peeled carrots, cut in small rounds. Leave everything to cook on a low heat and serve garnished with the chiles and olives. A colourful and appetising dish.

Gallina en Salsa de Chorizo
Broiler in Chorizo Sauce

A good and nourishing peasant dish, permeated by the spicy flavour of the chorizo.

1 *large broiler*	3 *chorizos (see p.* 17)
3 *cloves garlic*	2 *tablespoons oil*
1½ *onions*	10 *jalapeño chiles in vinegar*
Salt	

Singe the chicken, cut in pieces, wash and boil in water to cover with a clove of garlic, the ½ onion and salt. When it is tender (after about 1 hour), take the pieces out of the stock and allow to drain. Fry the remaining garlic and finely chopped onion and the chorizo in slices in the oil, then add the stock in which the chicken has been cooked, cover and leave to boil on a low light for 10 minutes. Add the pieces of chicken and the chiles in vinegar and serve piping hot with tortillas and Mexican white rice.

Pollo Bravo
Fiery Chicken

A lusciously piquant, highly coloured casserole.

1 *medium-sized chicken*	250 g (9 oz) tomatoes
1 *onion*	1 *dessertspoon powdered*
Salt	*piquín chile*
2 *cloves garlic*	250 g (9 oz) cooked peas
50 g (2 oz) lard	500 g (1 lb 2 oz) cooked small
500 g (1 lb 2 oz) Mexican	potatoes
green tomatoes (see p. 18)	

Singe the chicken, cut into pieces, wash and put to boil with the onion, salt and garlic. When it is cooked, take it out and dry thoroughly. Fry in hot lard. Put the green tomatoes on to boil, fry and peel the red tomatoes and grind with the garlic and onion. Dissolve the chile powder in a cup of the stock and put everything to dry in the fat, season with salt, add the peas and the chicken. Leave to boil until the sauce thickens. Serve with the potatoes, cut into strips and fried in lard. Follow with a green salad.

Pollo del Campesino
Farmhouse Chicken

Chicken in a thick, well-seasoned gravy.

1 *large chicken*	1 *handful shallots* or *spring*
Salt and pepper to taste	*onions*
1 *cup flour*	500 g (1 lb 2 oz) new potatoes
Oil for frying	1 *sprig parsley*
2 *cups water or stock*	

Cut the chicken into pieces, singe, wash well and dry with a damp cloth. Sprinkle with salt and pepper, turn in the flour, shake off excess flour and put the pieces in hot oil, one by one, until they are golden brown. Meanwhile, bring the water or stock to the boil and add the whole shallots or spring onions with a little of the leaf and the raw, scrubbed potatoes. When the potatoes are half cooked, add the pieces of chicken and continue cooking until everything is tender and there is a thick sauce. Serve with a robust green vegetable such as spinach or brussels sprouts.

Pollo en Salsa
Saucy Chicken

A fragrant dish, spicy and satisfying.

1 *large chicken*	2 *cloves garlic*
¾ *litre* (1¼ *pints*) *water*	2 *onions*
15 g (½ oz) *white bread*	2 *large red or green peppers*
5 *tablespoons lard*	4 *ancho chiles*
1 *stick cinnamon*	*Salt*
2 *cloves*	

Boil the chicken in the water until almost cooked (about 45 minutes). Remove from the stock. Fry the bread in the lard and grind with the spices, the garlic, the onions, the peppers and the fried, de-veined (previously soaked) chiles. Put all these ingredients into the stock in which you have boiled the chicken. Cut the chicken into pieces and fry in the remaining lard and when the stock comes up to the boil again, add the cooked chicken, season with salt and leave to boil until the sauce is good and thick. Serve with Mexican white rice and follow with a dressed green salad.

Pollo con Gabardina
Chicken in Batter

A quick and easy lunch dish with lots of flavour.

1 *medium-sized chicken*	1 *egg*
1 *cup flour*	1 *cup milk*
¼ *teaspoon baking powder*	3 *tablespoons butter*
Salt and pepper to taste	¾ *litre* (½ *pint*) *oil*
1 *teaspoon sugar*	

Singe the chicken, cut into pieces, wash and dry with a damp cloth. Mix the flour with the baking powder, salt, pepper and sugar in a deep bowl. Beat the egg lightly, add the milk and melted butter, mixing well and add to the flour little by little, beating well so that no lumps are formed. Dip the seasoned pieces of chicken in the batter, drain a little and fry in the hot oil at a regular heat so that they are golden brown on both sides. Remove from the oil and drain on a piece of absorbent paper. When all the chicken is fried, place on a large platter and put in a moderate oven for 20–25 minutes so that the chicken is properly cooked through. Serve with a tomato or green salad with vinaigrette dressing.

Pollo en su Jugo
Juicy Chicken

An attractive dish for a simple supper or lunch.

1 *large tender chicken*	50 g (2 oz) *olives*
150 g (5½ oz) *butter*	1 *lettuce*
2 *large cloves garlic*	*Salt and pepper to taste*
1 *pinch nutmeg*	

Singe, cut into pieces, wash, drain and dry the chicken with a damp cloth. Melt the butter in a casserole and brown the crushed garlic over a low light. When it is golden brown, remove the garlic from the casserole and throw it away. Fry the pieces of chicken in the garlic-flavoured butter, seasoning them with salt and pepper. Once the chicken is golden brown, sprinkle with nutmeg and add water to cover, adding more little by little until it is cooked. To serve, place a heap of lettuce in the centre of a large platter, put the pieces of chicken round the outside, pouring the sauce over them and decorating with the olives.

Pollo Elegante
Elegant Chicken

A sophisticated dish which is nonetheless inexpensive and easy to produce.

1 *tender chicken*	1 *cup white sauce*
250 g (9 oz) *peas*	2 *egg yolks*
500 g (1 lb 2 oz) *potatoes*	3 *tablespoons cream*
100 g (4 oz) *butter*	*Salt*
1 *cos lettuce*	

Singe the pieces of chicken, wash well, dry with a damp cloth and brown in the butter. Meanwhile, put the peas and potatoes on to boil and when cooked strain and peel the potatoes. In another pot, toss the peas in 1 tablespoon of the butter and remove. Toss the well-washed and dried lettuce leaves in the butter without over-cooking; place them in the bottom of a flat casserole or mould. Put the pieces of chicken on top of the lettuce and pour over the white sauce. Sprinkle the peas over the top.

Mash the potatoes, add the 2 egg yolks, 2 tablespoons of the butter, the cream and season with salt. Decorate the edge of the dish containing the chicken with the mashed potato, using a forcing pipe, if available. Brown in a hot oven or under the grill and serve immediately.

Pato en Jugo de Naranja
Duck in Orange Sauce

Duck and orange are a traditionally well-matched pair. Here, the duck is slowly casseroled in the orange juice, which tenderises and gives added savour to the meat.

1 *duck*	¾ *litre (1¼ pints) fresh orange*
2 *onions*	*juice*
2 *cloves garlic*	¼ *litre (½ pint) vinegar*
4 *tomatoes*	2 *bay leaves*
1 *sprig parsley*	1 *sprig thyme*
30 g *(1 oz) raisins*	1 *sprig marjoram*
50 g *(2 oz) blanched almonds*	*Salt to taste*

Cut the duck into smallish pieces and place in an earthenware or heavy-bottomed casserole. Add the finely chopped onion, garlic, tomatoes and parsley with the raisins, thinly sliced almonds, orange juice, vinegar, herbs and salt. Cover the pot with a close-fitting heavy lid – if earthenware, seal the rims with a heavy flour paste, if metal, wrap a cloth round the lid before placing it on the casserole, to prevent any liquid escaping during cooking. Shake the pot from time to time to prevent sticking but DO NOT open the lid. Cook over a very low heat on an asbestos mat for 3 hours. Serve the duck hot with the juice poured over it, accompanied by Mexican white rice and a green salad.

Pichones a la Antigua
Pigeons Cooked the Old-fashioned Way

A touch of sherry and an almond sauce give this dish a sumptuous, mellow flavour.

3 *pigeons*	*Salt and pepper*
2 *small onions*	1 *tablespoon lard*
4 *tablespoons white wine*	50 g *(2 oz) almonds*

1 *hard-boiled egg yolk*
50 g (2 oz) *ham*
2 *cloves*
1 *peppercorn*

250 g (9 oz) *tomatoes*
50 g (2 oz) *cooked green peas*
5 *tablespoons sherry*

Boil the pigeons in water to cover with 1 sliced onion, the white wine, salt and pepper.

Fry the unblanched almonds in the lard and grind with the hard-boiled egg yolk, half of the ham and the spices. Add this to the pigeon stock. In the fat used to fry the almonds, fry the rest of the ham and the cooked pigeons. Add the tomatoes, previously puréed with the other onion. When this dries, add the pigeon stock, containing the almonds, egg yolks, etc., and leave to simmer until thick. Add the sherry and peas. Boil up once and serve with Mexican white rice.

Pichones Encebollados
Pigeon with Onions

In this recipe the white wine and root vegetables admirably complement the slightly smoky flavour of the meat.

3 *pigeons*
10 *very small onions*
3 *carrots*
3 *turnips*
1 *tablespoon chopped parsley*
50 g (2 oz) *bacon*

½ *teaspoon grated nutmeg*
Salt and pepper to taste
¼ *litre (½ pint) stock*
½ *glass white wine*
Lard or oil for frying
Fried bread

Place the pigeons in a large deep casserole and arrange round them the whole onions, rings of carrot, turnips, chopped parsley, chopped bacon, salt, pepper and nutmeg. Pour over the stock and wine and allow to simmer until the birds are tender (45–50 minutes). Meanwhile, fry pieces of bread and place them on a large serving dish. Place the halved pigeons on the pieces of fried bread and garnish with the onions, turnips and carrots.

Meat

One very rarely sees lamb or mutton sold in Mexico, though whole roast young kid is considered a delicacy. Most of the recipes given here are for beef and pork.

Puchero
Mexican Pot au Feu

This is a Yucatecan dish to which an entire ritual of eating and serving is attached. I was lucky enough to be taught the old traditions by a charming elderly Yucatecan lady, the *abuelita* of a friend of ours. A tasty dish and one which is especially good if you are feeding a lot of people, as it is prepared well in advance. Soup, meat and vegetables are all cooked in the same large casserole and it does not spoil by being cooked longer than planned. This recipe will serve 10.

100 g (4 oz) chick-peas
500 g (1 lb 2 oz) beef
500 g (1 lb 2 oz) pork
1 marrow bone
1 chicken
3 onions
3 cloves garlic
10 black peppercorns
3 corns on the cob
1 small cabbage
4 turnips
6 courgettes

4 carrots
4 tablespoons tomato purée
  (p. 18)
Salt and pepper
3 peaches
3 pears
500 g (1 lb 2 oz) potatoes (or
  250 g (9 oz) potatoes and
  250 g (9 oz) sweet potato
  if available)
50 g (2 oz) lard
2 large bananas

For the garnish:
Coriander leaf
2 lemons
5 avocados

1 bunch radishes
1 cucumber
Salt and pepper

You will need a large-capacity earthenware casserole or preserving pan to make this dish.

Soak the chick-peas overnight. The following day, boil in 4 litres (7 pints) of water with the whole chunks of beef and pork, the marrow bone, the chicken cut in large quarters, 1 onion, the garlic and the peppercorns. When it comes to the boil, skim. When the meat is tender, after an hour and a half, add the corn on the cob, cut in thirds, the cabbage, chopped into large chunks, the turnips, the sliced courgettes, cut in quarters, the whole carrots, the tomato purée and salt to taste. Leave to boil till they are tender, about 40 minutes. Meanwhile, boil the peaches and pears in a separate pan. Slice, peel and fry the potatoes in lard. Peel the bananas, slice and fry them also till they are crisp. Reserve these and add them to the vegetable plate.

To serve: Remove the meat, vegetables and marrow bone from the stock and place on separate platters, leaving the vegetables whole but cutting the meat so that everyone can have a piece of each sort. Remove the marrow from the bone and add to the meat platter.

Serve the hot soup in separate bowls garnished with chopped coriander leaf, a wedge of lemon and some diced avocado. The soup can be eaten as a first course or along with the main course.

On a bed of Mexican white rice (see p. 38), everyone should serve themselves a good selection of meat and vegetables. Before eating, all the ingredients should be chopped up small and liberally sprinkled with pieces of chopped radish and cucumber chopped in chunks sprinkled with salt, allowed to soak and then drained. Tortillas should be eaten with the meal, strips being taken off and used as a small shovel on to which the meat and vegetables are scooped and popped into the mouth.

Picadillo
Mexican Minced Meat

A personal favourite, being inexpensive and easy to prepare, a highly spiced and delicious combination of meat with almonds, raisins, bananas and candied citron.

1 *onion*	2 *small bananas*
750 g (1¾ *lb*) *minced meat*	50 g (2 *oz*) *olives*
(½ *pork*, ½ *beef*)	6 *pickled chiles*
Lard	1 *tablespoon chopped parsley*
1 *cup tomato purée* (*p. 18*)	1 *stick cinnamon*
4 *small potatoes, cut in small*	2 *cloves*
cubes (*optional*)	1 *tablespoon sugar*
50 g (2 *oz*) *almonds*	*Bay leaf and thyme*
50 g (2 *oz*) *raisins*	*Salt and pepper*
50 g (2 *oz*) *candied citron*	

Brown the chopped onion and the meat in lard: the meat should be cooked till hard. Add the tomato purée. When this is thick, add the parboiled potatoes (if desired), the blanched, sliced almonds, the raisins, diced candied citron, banana, cut in rounds, olives, chopped chiles and the parsley. Season with cinnamon, cloves, sugar, bay leaf, thyme, salt and pepper. Leave to simmer on a low heat until the mixture is thick and the meat is thoroughly cooked. Serve with Mexican white rice and tortillas.

Albondigas
Mexican Meat Balls

Mexicans eat meat balls in a highly spiced tomato sauce, scooped up on tortillas.

250 g (9 *oz*) *minced beef*	1 *onion*
250 g (9 *oz*) *minced pork*	50 g (2 *oz*) *bread, soaked in*
250 g (9 *oz*) *minced lamb*	*milk*

4 *eggs*
100 *g (4 oz) ham*

50 *g (2 oz) olives*
Salt and pepper

For the sauce:
50 *g (2 oz) bread*
4 *tablespoons lard*
1 *onion*
3 *pickled chipotle chiles*
1 *sprig coriander leaf*
1 *sprig parsley*

¼ *cup vinegar*
500 *g (1 lb 2 oz) Mexican*
green tomatoes
Salt and pepper
1 *litre (1¾ pints) stock*

Mince the meats together with the onion and the soaked bread. Add 2 beaten raw eggs, 2 chopped, hard-boiled eggs, diced ham and olives. Season with salt and pepper. Blend the mixture well, form into small balls the size of a walnut and place these on a floured board to rest for half an hour.

To make the sauce: Fry and grind the bread with the onion, chiles, coriander leaf, parsley and vinegar. Add the green tomatoes, season with salt and pepper and when this thickens, add the stock. When this begins to boil, add the meat balls and continue cooking until they are all tender. Serve in the stock with Mexican white rice and tortillas.

Rollo de Carne
Mexican Meat Loaf

An attractive dish, the filling of which can be varied according to imagination and your family's likes.

For the loaf
1 *onion*
750 *g (1¾ lb) minced beef*
50 *g (2 oz) breadcrumbs*

Herbs (mint, thyme and bay
leaf or sage) to taste
2 *eggs*
Salt and pepper

Chop the onion finely and mix with the minced beef, the breadcrumbs, herbs, the beaten eggs and salt and pepper. Roll out on a board in a long rectangle.

For the filling: This is where you can invent with what you have in the cupboard – colour is important here. The following filling works well.

2 *hard-boiled eggs*	100 g (4 oz) *ham or spicy*
250 g (9 oz) *carrots*	*sausage*
250 g (9 oz) *peas or green*	*Salt and pepper* \
beans	

Boil the eggs and vegetables and chop them finely. Add the chopped ham, season with salt and pepper and mix well. Place the filling along the middle of the rectangular meat mixture and roll into a long sausage shape, place it on a piece of aluminium foil, secure this firmly all round and cook in boiling water for an hour. Remove from the water and open the foil. Leave to cool for a few minutes. Then cut into small slices. Arrange the rounds on a warmed plate. Serve with a mixed or green salad, with a tomato sauce or Oscar's Special Pâté Sauce (p. 25).

Lomo de Cerdo Adobado
Pueblan Pork Loin

Deliciously spicy, this recipe is a very good way to serve the less expensive cuts of pork, such as belly.

1 *kg* (2¼ *lb*) *pork loin or belly*	*Salt*
250 g (9 oz) *ancho chile or*	⅛ *litre* (¼ *pint*) *vinegar*
1 *tablespoon chile powder*	1 *tablespoon oregano*
6 *cloves garlic*	1 *sprig thyme*
6 *peppercorns*	2 *bay leaves*
10 *cumin seeds*	3 *mint leaves*
1 *stick cinnamon*	100 g (4 oz) *lard*

For garnish:

1 *onion*	1 *lettuce*
50 g (2 oz) *olives*	6 *pickled chiles*
6 *radishes*	

Wash the pork and cut in thick strips. Place in a casserole
and marinade overnight with the de-veined chiles, soaked
and ground with the garlic, peppercorns, cumin seeds,
cinnamon, salt, vinegar, oregano, thyme, bay leaves and
mint leaves. The following day, add the lard and place on a
hot flame, turning the meat frequently so that it does not
burn. When it is well browned, add half a pint of water and
leave to simmer until very little sauce remains. Take out the
pieces of meat and place on a warmed platter, pouring the
sauce over it. Garnish with onion rings, olives, radishes,
lettuce and small pickled chiles.

Lomo de Puerco Mechado
Spiked Pork Loin

Pot roast with a difference! The loin is permeated by the
flavour of the herbs and spices with which it is studded and
smothered in a tomato sauce.

1 *large onion*	750 g (1¾ *lb*) *pork loin*
1½ *tablespoons chopped parsley*	4 *tablespoons lard or oil for frying*
150 g (5½ oz) *ham*	6 *tomatoes*
2 *cloves*	*Salt and pepper*
1 *stick cinnamon*	24 *olives*
6 *peppercorns*	

Chop the onion very finely and mix with the parsley. Cut the
ham in very narrow strips. Grind the cloves, cinnamon and
peppercorns. With the point of a knife or a skewer, make
several deep holes on all sides of the meat and fill these with
the onion and parsley, topping up with the strips of ham
sprinkled with the spices.

Heat the lard in a casserole and fry the meat so that it is
well browned all over. Add the peeled, ground tomatoes and

add ½ litre (1 pint) of water. Cook for an hour and a half and when the stock is thick, season with salt and pepper, add the olives and serve.

Lomo Enchilado
Chiled Pork Loin

Pork in a chile sauce, thickened and mellowed with potatoes.

6 *ancho chiles*   1 *kg* (2¼ *lb*) *pork loin*
2 *cloves garlic*   2 *tablespoons oil or lard*
Salt to taste   12 *medium-sized potatoes*

Soak the chiles overnight without toasting. Grind with the garlic and salt. Brown the meat in the lard and add the ground chile mixture, browning well. Add 1 litre (1¾ pints) of water and when the pork is tender, add the potatoes, peeled and cut in quarters. Leave to simmer till very little thick sauce is left and serve with tortillas and a mixed salad.

Estofado de Res
Beef Stew

Liven up a beef stew by adding poblano chile (or green pepper and a pinch of chile powder) and tomatoes.

750 *g* (1¾ *lb*) *stewing steak*   5 *large tomatoes*
4 *tablespoons oil or lard for*   2 *onions*
   frying   4 *poblano chiles* (or 2 *large*
1 *sprig thyme*   *green peppers and pinch of*
1 *bay leaf*   *chile*)
Salt and pepper to taste   9 *medium-sized potatoes*

Cut the meat into smallish pieces and brown in lard. Mix in the herbs and add ½ litre (1 pint) stock or water with salt and pepper to taste. Add the tomatoes, onions and chiles. Leave to cook for 45 minutes on a low light with a close-fitting lid. Then add the peeled, quartered potatoes. Cook for a further

30 minutes or until the meat and potatoes are thoroughly cooked and the liquid has reduced to a thick sauce. Serve with side dishes of beans, tortillas and Mexican white rice.

Carne Picada con Rajas
Minced Meat with Strips of Chile

A quick, inexpensive and tasty *picadillo*.

400 g (14 oz) potatoes	4 tablespoons lard
8 poblano chiles (or	2 small onions
4 green peppers with chile	750 g (1¾ lb) minced beef
powder to taste)	Salt and pepper to taste
5 large tomatoes	

Boil the potatoes; fry, de-vein and cut the chiles into strips. Fry and grind the tomatoes.

In very hot fat, fry the finely chopped onion and as it goes golden brown, add the strips of chile and after a few minutes, add the minced beef and fry till it is brown but not hard. Add the tomato purée, salt and pepper and leave to simmer for 5 minutes. Add the cooked, peeled and quartered potatoes. Cook for a few minutes longer and serve with beans and tortillas.

Rollos de Filete a la Mexicana
Mexican-style Beef Olives

A colourful and tasty dish of Spanish origin.

1 kg (2¼ lb) frying steak	3 hard-boiled eggs
250 g (9 oz) peas (shelled)	100 g (4 oz) bacon
250 g (9 oz) green beans	2 tablespoons lard or oil for
3 medium-sized carrots	frying
1 small onion	Salt and pepper to taste

Buy a long strip of steak about 1 cm (½ in) thick. Boil the peas, beans and carrots in salted water and then chop and mix them together with the finely chopped onion, egg, salt and pepper. Place the rashers of bacon crosswise down the piece of meat and on top of this place the filling. Roll up the piece of meat with the filling inside and secure with tooth-picks. Then cut strips about 4 cm (1½ in) long, tying each roll with a piece of thread. Heat the lard or oil and fry the steak on all sides till well browned. Cover and put in the oven or on a very low heat for a further 20 minutes. Serve very hot, removing tooth-picks and thread, with *salsa roja* (see p. 128), tortillas, Mexican white rice and beans.

Asado de Ternera con Perejil
Veal Stew with Capers and Parsley

An attractive and subtly flavoured dish.

750 g (1¾ lb) veal	Bay leaf and rosemary to
Salt and pepper to taste	taste
9 cloves garlic	3 tablespoons vinegar
2 tablespoons lard	36 capers
1 large onion	24 olives
3 tablespoons chopped parsley	

The piece of veal should be seasoned with salt and pieces of garlic poked into it with the aid of a sharp knife or skewer. Fry in the lard with slices of onion, plenty of chopped parsley and a sprinkling of herbs. When the meat is golden brown on all sides, add the vinegar. Cover the casserole and add a little water or stock. Cook for an hour, after which the sauce should be thick and the meat well cooked. Garnish the meat with capers, olives and onion rings and serve piping hot with Mexican white rice and beans.

Conejo Almendrado
Rabbit with Almonds

A deliciously tender rabbit casserole, with a rich almond sauce containing tomatoes, peas and potatoes.

1 *large tender rabbit*
1 *cup vinegar*
1 *large and* 1 *small onion*
3 *tablespoons lard or oil*
1 *slice of bread*
100 g (4 *oz*) *almonds*

500 g (1 *lb* 2 *oz*) *tomatoes*
Bay leaf and thyme
Salt and pepper to taste
500 g (1 *lb* 2 *oz*) *peas*
250 g (9 *oz*) *potatoes*

Cut the rabbit in pieces and marinade overnight in a large casserole with the cup of vinegar and a large sliced onion. The following day, brown the rabbit in lard and then boil with the vinegar and onion in which it was marinaded in lightly salted water.

When it is cooked but not very tender (after about 30 minutes), remove it from the stock, drain well and fry it again in oil. In the same oil, fry a slice of bread, the small onion (sliced), the unpeeled almonds and finally the whole tomatoes. The almonds, bread, onion and tomato should be ground, adding the herbs and salt and pepper to taste.

Place the pieces of rabbit in a casserole and pour the sauce over them, adding a little of the water in which the rabbit was boiled. Allow to simmer for a few minutes, then add the previously cooked peas and potatoes cut in small pieces. Leave to heat well through, so that the flavours mingle and serve piping hot with tortillas.

Note: 4 tablespoons of capers may be used in place of the almonds. Half should be ground with the bread, onion and tomato, half should be kept whole and added to the casserole 5 minutes before serving. The flavour of capers complements that of the meat particularly well. The dish is then called *Conejo Alcaparrado*.

Vegetables and Salads

At a Mexican *tianguis* (movable market) you can see the marvellously vast choice of weird and wonderful vegetables which are at the disposal of the Mexican housewife. These range from the vegetables which can be grown in the temperate, mountainous zones to tropical and desert species. Some, such as *nopalitos* (prickly pear leaves) and *romeritos* (a plant similar to rosemary which is used as a vegetable), are difficult to find in Britain. I include recipes for vegetables which are commonly found at your local greengrocer or delicatessen.

There are many recipes for stuffed chiles. Here are a few of them.

Chiles Rellenos
Stuffed Chiles

Traditionally, the poblano chiles are stuffed with a spicy minced meat **picadillo**, dipped in batter, deep fried and served in a tomato stock.

250g (9 oz) tomatoes
50 g (2 oz) almonds
50 g (2 oz) candied citron
250 g (9 oz) minced veal or beef
250 g (9 oz) minced pork
1 onion
2 tablespoons lard

50 g (2 oz) pine nuts
2 tablespoons vinegar
1 tablespoon sugar
½ teaspoon ground cinnamon
Salt and pepper to taste
12 poblano chiles (or 12 smallish green peppers)
1 sprig parsley

For the coating
4 eggs
4 tablespoons flour

250 g (9 oz) lard

For the stock:

750 g (1¾ lb) tomatoes

1 onion

1 stick cinnamon

1 tablespoon lard

¼ litre (½ pint) meat stock

Salt and pepper

Purée the tomatoes. Blanch and slice the almonds. Dice the candied citron. Sauté the minced meat and finely chopped onion in 2 tablespoons of lard. Add the tomato purée, almonds, citron and pine nuts. Season with vinegar, sugar, ground cinnamon, salt and pepper and leave to simmer on a low heat till thick. Toast the chiles, leave them to sweat wrapped in a damp cloth for 30 minutes. Then skin, slit, remove veins and seeds and stuff with the meat mixture. Dip each stuffed chile in flour, then in beaten egg and fry in deep fat. When the chiles are golden brown, remove from the fat, drain and place in the prepared stock. Leave to simmer briefly and serve sprinkled with chopped parsley.

If you are using green peppers, cut a little hat off the top, remove the seeds and proceed to stuff with the meaty mixture. You do not have to cover the peppers with batter and deep-fry as this is done to counteract the piquancy of the chile, but you will have to cook them for longer in the stock – about 1 hour.

To make the stock: Purée the tomatoes with the onion and stick of cinnamon. Strain and sauté in 1 tablespoon of lard. Add the meat stock, salt and pepper. When this has thickened a little, add the fried chiles.

Chiles Rellenos de Elote
Chiles Stuffed with Sweet Corn

A colourful vegetable accompaniment to a meat course, which can also be eaten as a main meal, doubling the quantities for 6 persons. A tasty dish and especially useful if any of your guests are vegetarian.

12 *large poblano chiles or*
   6 green peppers
3 *tender corns on the cob or*
   1 large tin sweet corn
250 g *(9 oz) mild cheddar*
   cheese

1 *small onion*
1 *sprig coriander leaf or*
   parsley
½ *litre (1 pint) white sauce*

Toast and peel the chiles. Scrape the kernels from the cobs and cook for 30 minutes or heat the contents of a large tin of sweet corn. Drain the kernels well and mix with half of the grated cheese, the finely chopped onion and chopped coriander leaf or parsley. Make a slit in the side of the chiles, remove the veins and seeds and stuff with the mixture. Place the chiles in a large flat casserole and pour over the hot white sauce. Leave over a very low heat for a few minutes, then serve, garnished with the rest of the grated cheese.

Chiles Rellenos de Frijoles
Chiles Stuffed with Beans

Another delicious and very nutritious vegetarian meal or accompaniment to a meat course. Double the quantities for 6 persons if it is to be served as the main dish.

700 g *(1¼ lb) kidney beans*
¼ *litre (½ pint) oil*
1 *cup tomato purée (p. 18)*
1 *onion*
½ *teaspoon oregano*
Salt to taste

12 *poblano chiles or 6 green*
   peppers
4 *eggs*
4 *tablespoons flour*
¼ *litre (½ pint) cream*
100 g *(4 oz) butter*
100 g *(4 oz) cheese*

Boil the beans as usual (see p. 15). Mash and sauté in half the oil with the tomato purée, chopped onion, oregano and salt. Leave to simmer until thick.

Toast, skin and clean the chiles by making a slit in the side. Fill with the bean mixture, dip in a batter made from the beaten eggs and flour and fry in the oil. Place the stuffed chiles on absorbent paper to drain, then arrange them in a greased baking dish. Pour the cream over the chiles, dot with butter and sprinkle the grated cheese on top. Put in a moderate oven for about 30 minutes until lightly browned. Serve immediately with tortillas and a green salad.

Chiles Rellenos en Nogada
Stuffed Chiles in Walnut Sauce

A luscious combination of hot chiles and mellow walnuts, attractively garnished with pomegranate seeds. Double the quantities for a main meal for 6.

12 *poblano chiles or* 6 *green peppers*	50 g (2 oz) *sultanas*
1 *onion*	*Salt and pepper*
250 g (9 oz) *minced pork*	1 *pomegranate*
50 g (2 oz) *almonds*	1 *tablespoon chopped parsley*

For the sauce:

50 *walnuts*	3 *cumin seeds*
50 g (2 oz) *pumpkin seeds*	2 *cloves*
250 g (9 oz) *fresh cheese*	*Salt*
4 *cloves garlic*	

To make the walnut sauce: Shell the nuts, wash and soak them overnight in cold water. Grind. Wash the pumpkin seeds to remove the green outer covering and grind with the cheese, the fried cloves of garlic, cumin seed and cloves. Mix well, adding salt to taste.

Toast the chiles, skin and stuff with a *picadillo* made by frying the finely chopped onion, adding the minced pork, the chopped almonds and the sultanas. Add salt and pepper and simmer for 10 minutes. Pour the walnut sauce over the stuffed chiles and garnish with the pomegranate seeds and chopped parsley.

Chiles Rellenos Estilo Arriero
Muleteers' Stuffed Chiles

Chiles stuffed with peas and tomatoes, smothered in melted cheese. A light vegetable dish, delicious with chicken or pork.

12 *poblano chiles or* 6 *green peppers*	2 *small tomatoes*
	Salt
500 g (1 lb 2 oz) *green peas*	4 *tablespoons lard or oil*
1 *onion*	200 g (7 oz) *grated parmesan*
2 *cloves garlic*	

Toast the chiles, remove the skin, slit down the side, devein and remove the seeds. Cook the peas and mix with the finely chopped onion, garlic and tomatoes, seasoning with salt. Fry the mixture in lard or oil and stuff the chiles with it. Place in a casserole and sprinkle with grated cheese and oil. Put in a moderate oven for 30 minutes or until the cheese has melted.

Calabacitas a la Mexicana
Courgettes Mexican Style

A scrumptious slimmer's lunch or vegetable side dish. Double the quantities if it is to be served as a main dish for 6.

1 kg (2¼ lb) *medium-sized courgettes*	3 *tablespoons lard or oil*
	1 *small onion*
250 g (9 oz) *pork loin or belly*	2 *medium-sized tomatoes*
2 *poblano chiles (or* 1 *large green pepper)*	1 *clove garlic*
	Salt and pepper to taste
2 *corns on the cob (or* 1 *cob and* 1 *small tin sweet corn)*	250 g (9 oz) *cheese*

Dice the courgettes and pork. Fry the chiles, cut in strips. Cut one cob of corn into rounds and scrape the kernels off the other. Brown the meat in the hot lard and add the finely chopped onion, tomato and garlic. Finally add the courgettes, the strips of chile and the corn. Season with salt and pepper and leave to simmer in its own juice for 30 minutes. Serve with strips of cheese.

Tortas de Coliflor
Cauliflower Fritters

Cauliflower responds well to imaginative cooking and these fritters are a personal favourite, served with a main meat dish or savoury cheese pie.

1 *medium-sized cauliflower*	*Salt and pepper*
100 g (4 oz) *cheese*	*Lard or oil for frying*
½ *cup flour*	5 *medium-sized tomatoes*
2 *eggs*	1 *small onion*

Wash the cauliflower and separate into small flowerets. Boil for 4 minutes and drain well. Cut the cheese into little sticks and place a stick in the centre of each piece of cauliflower. Sprinkle with some flour. Beat the egg whites until they rise in peaks, then add the beaten egg yolks, a tablespoon of flour and salt and pepper. Drench the pieces of cauliflower in this and fry in very hot fat.

Make a stock with the tomatoes, boiling them in a little water, then peeling them and passing them through a sieve. Fry the onion in a little fat and when it is golden brown, add the tomato purée and salt to taste. Leave to simmer until thickened, then pour over the hot fritters and serve immediately.

Tortas de Camote
Sweet Potato Fritters

Savoury fritters, served as a starter, an accompaniment to a quiche or as a main course, doubling the quantities for 6.

500 g (1 *lb* 2 *oz*) sweet
  potato
1 *small onion*
5 *tablespoons lard or oil*
250 g (9 *oz*) pork
2 *tablespoons sultanas*

1 *tablespoon chopped almonds*
Salt and pepper
3 *tablespoons flour*
3 *eggs*
1 *litre* (1¾ *pints*) meat stock
4 *medium-sized tomatoes*

Choose medium-sized tender sweet potatoes to avoid a
fibrous result. Cook, peel and cut into slices of about 1 cm
(½ in) thick. Brown the onion in hot lard, dice the meat and
add to the fat along with the sultanas and almonds. Add salt
and pepper and allow to simmer for a few minutes.

Take a slice of sweet potato, add a little of the *picadillo*
(minced meat mixture), then place another slice of sweet
potato on top. Sprinkle with flour. Add a tablespoon of
flour to the beaten egg and season with salt and pepper.
Cover the sweet potato and meat sandwich with the batter
and fry in very hot lard, taking care that the fritters do not
disintegrate. When they are golden brown, remove from the
fat and drain on absorbent paper. Then add to the meat
stock with the ground tomatoes and a little chopped onion
added to it. Serve immediately piping hot.

Tortas de Ejote
Green Bean Fritters

A tasty way of using up left-over green beans.

500 g (1 *lb* 2 *oz*) green beans
2 *eggs*
1 *tablespoon flour*
½ *teaspoon nutmeg*

Salt to taste
4 *tablespoons lard or oil*
3 *large tomatoes*
1 *small onion*

Prepare and cook the beans till tender. Drain well. Beat the
eggs, add the flour, nutmeg and a little salt. Take up small
handfuls of beans, dip in the egg mixture and fry in very hot
lard. Leave to drain on absorbent paper. Then add to a sauce

made with the peeled, ground tomatoes and finely chopped
brown onion. Season with salt and pepper. Allow to simmer
for a few minutes and serve piping hot.

Col Rellena
Stuffed Cabbage

A favourite dish in most European countries, the addition
of almonds, sultanas and candied citron gives the Mexican
version an added exoticism. It gains, too, by being quick and
simple to prepare.

1 *medium cabbage*	50 g (2 oz) *sultanas*
250 g (9 oz) *minced pork*	50 g (2 oz) *candied citron*
2 *tablespoons oil*	25 g (1 oz) *almonds*
1 *clove garlic*	200 g (7 oz) *bacon*
1 *small onion*	1 *tablespoon flour*
1 *small tomato*	2 *cups meat stock*
Bay leaf and thyme	*Salt and pepper*

Wash the cabbage and plunge it whole into plenty of boiling
salted water. Cover and cook for 10 minutes, draining well.
  Meanwhile, make the *picadillo* or minced meat filling.
Brown the meat in oil, then the garlic, finely chopped onion
and tomato. Add the herbs, simmer till dry, then add the
sultanas, candied citron, blanched chopped almonds and a
little sugar if desired. When the cabbage is cool enough to
handle, open out the outer leaves and cut out and remove
the hard centre part. Fill the hollowed-out cabbage with
some of the *picadillo*. Take a casserole slightly larger than
the cabbage. Cover the bottom with long strips of bacon,
place the cabbage on these, opening the outer leaves and
stuffing the gap between each couple of leaves with *picadillo*,
pulling up the leaves into the cabbage form and securing
them at the top with the pieces of bacon which should be
long enough to stretch right round the cabbage. Secure with
tooth-picks. Brown the flour in a little oil. Add the stock,

salt and pepper to taste and stir well and leave to simmer for a few minutes. Pour over the cabbage. Place in a hot oven for 1 hour, basting from time to time. Serve with Mexican white rice.

Colecitas de Bruselas con Tocino
Brussels Sprouts with Bacon

Give brussels a new lease of life, tossed in a bacon and tomato sauce.

500 g (1 *lb* 2 *oz*) *brussels*   1 *cup tomato purée* (*p.* 18)
  sprouts   *Salt and pepper to taste*
100 g (4 *oz*) *bacon*

Prepare the sprouts and cook them for 7 minutes in boiling, salted water. Drain well. Dice the bacon and brown. Toss the sprouts in the same fat with the bacon, then add the tomato purée, salt and pepper. Leave to simmer for a few minutes and serve very hot.

Colecitas de Bruselas con Crema
Brussels Sprouts with Cream

A touch of luxury – sprouts in cream topped with melted cheese.

500 g (1 *lb* 2 *oz*) *brussels*   *Salt and pepper to taste*
  sprouts   1 *small cup single cream*
1 *tablespoon butter*   100 g (4 *oz*) *cheese*
1 *small onion*

Prepare the sprouts and cook for 7 minutes in salted boiling water. Melt the butter in a saucepan, fry the finely chopped onion till golden brown. Toss the sprouts in the butter and onion and season with salt and pepper. Add the cream and sprinkle the cheese on top. Pop in the oven or under the grill for a moment to brown the cheese.

Croquetas de Espinaca
Spinach Croquettes

Spinach with a difference. Children will eat up their greens if they are done like this in bite-sized croquettes with a piece of cheese in the middle.

500 g (1 lb 2 oz) spinach   100 g (4 oz) cheese
2 eggs   Salt and pepper to taste
2 tablespoons flour

Cook the spinach. Drain very well, pressing so that all the water is forced out. Chop very finely. Beat the eggs and add them with the flour to the spinach. Mix thoroughly. Cut the cheese into small sticks. Take up a spoonful of the spinach mixture, push a piece of cheese into the centre of it. Form into a croquette and fry in very hot lard. Serve very hot with Mexican white rice, a meat dish or savoury pie or as a starter on their own.

Timbalitos de Espinacas
Spinach Moulds

Sophisticated spinach. These individual moulds make a delicious dish on their own with rice or liven up a cold meat platter. Double the quantities if it is to be served as a main course for 6.

500 g (1 lb 2 oz) spinach   200 g (7 oz) bacon or ham
2 tablespoons butter   1 small onion
2 tablespoons cream or milk   2 hard-boiled eggs
1 egg   Salt and pepper

Wash the spinach thoroughly. Cook, drain very thoroughly and chop finely. Mix with the butter, cream or milk, raw egg, salt and pepper. Butter 6 individual moulds and fill with the tightly packed spinach mixture. Place to cook in a *bain marie* in a moderate oven for 30 minutes or until the egg has set.

Turn out on a warm plate, surround each mould with a rasher of browned bacon or piece of ham and garnish with strips of hard-boiled egg. One large mould can be used, turned out and garnished with the bacon and hard-boiled eggs.

SALADS

Ensalada Mexicana
Mexican Salad

The most common Mexican salad, served after the meat course and beans.

1 *lettuce*	1 *tablespoon lemon juice*
4 *large tomatoes*	1 *clove garlic*
3 *avocados*	½ *teaspoon mustard*
3 *tablespoons oil*	*Salt and pepper*

Shred the lettuce roughly, slice the tomatoes and peeled avocados. Mix the oil, lemon juice, crushed garlic, mustard, salt and pepper. Pour the dressing over the salad, toss and serve.

Ensalada de Jitomates
Tomato Salad

An attractive finish or start to a meal.

6 *large tomatoes*	3 *large avocados*
Oil and vinegar to taste	200 g (7 oz) *ham*
Salt and pepper	

Slice the tomatoes, place on a large platter and sprinkle with salt, pepper, oil and vinegar. Chop the avocados and mix with the chopped ham. Serve, covering each slice of tomato completely with the avocado and ham mixture.

Coliflor con Aguacate
Cauliflower in Avocado

Cauliflower smothered in an avocado and almond paste. A luxurious and colourful accompaniment to a hot or cold meal.

1 *large cauliflower*
2 *tablespoons vinegar*
3 *tablespoons oil*
Salt, pepper and nutmeg to
  taste

4 *large avocados*
100 *g (4 oz) ground almonds*
10 *tiny radishes*

Wash the cauliflower thoroughly, trimming the central stalk and place it whole in plenty of salted boiling water. When it is tender, drain well and leave to cool. Drench it in vinegar, oil, salt and pepper and place on a round plate. Mash the avocados with the ground almonds, salt, pepper and nutmeg. Spread this paste all over the cauliflower and garnish with the radishes.

Ensalada de Calabacitas
Courgette Salad

A subtly flavoured salad, suitable to be served with fish or cold platters.

500 *g (1 lb 2 oz) small tender*
  courgettes
Oil and vinegar to taste

1 *tablespoon oregano*
50 *g (2 oz) cheese*
Salt to taste

Boil the courgettes in lightly salted water. Slice lengthwise, then in halves or quarters and leave to cool. When they are cold, add oil and vinegar to taste, the oregano and the grated or crumbled cheese with a little salt. A few slivers of onion may be added if desired.

Ensalada Tricolor
Mexican Flag Salad

An appetising hors d'oeuvre or refreshing finish to a meal.

5 *tender corns on the cob* or   2 *tablespoons vinegar*
    2 *large tins sweet corn*   ½ *cup oil*
2 *egg yolks*   5 *pomegranates*
Salt and pepper   5 *avocados*

Boil the corn cobs till tender and scrape off the kernels.
Drain the kernels well. Make a mayonnaise by beating the
egg yolks, beating in salt, pepper and vinegar, then adding
the oil drop by drop very slowly, beating continually (see
also p. 131). Combine the mayonnaise with the corn kernels
and heap them up in the centre of a flat plate. Surround with
a ring of pomegranate seeds and another of avocado slices
to give the colours of the Mexican flag.

Beans

With the growing awareness that vegetables are more economical than meat in terms of the amount of protein produced to the hectares of land needed to produce it, more people are turning to pulses, such as beans and lentils. Beans provide almost all the proteins adults need and the amount of meat served can thus be reduced except in the case of growing children.

The traditional Mexican diet of maize and beans, with chiles for flavour and meat when it is available, is a balanced and very nutritious one. It is interesting, too, that the centuries-old method of *intercropping*, growing the beans amongst the maize, has proved most efficient, though impossible to mechanise, because the maize provides support for the bean plants and the beans provide nitrates for the maize.

Beans are always eaten in Mexico after the meat course rather than in a stew with the meat. You may wish to try both methods.

Frijoles Estilo Mexicano
Mexican-style Beans

Cooking time: 4 hours.

500 g (1 *lb* 2 *oz*) *black,*   2 *cloves garlic*
    black-eyed, pink or red   4 *tablespoons lard*
    kidney beans   *Salt*
2 *onions*

Clean the beans, removing any stones or other foreign matter. Wash them well and soak overnight in cold water. The following day, put the beans to boil in an earthenware pot, making up the amount of soaking water to 2 litres

(3½ pints). Add the quartered onions and the cloves of garlic. Simmer gently and when the skins of the beans begin to wrinkle, add the lard. As liquid is absorbed, add more hot (never cold) water. After about 3½ hours or when the beans are almost done, add salt. Continue cooking for another 30 minutes and serve hot with a little of their juice after the meat course. The juice may be thickened by removing ½ cup of the beans, mashing them and returning them to the casserole, allowing the beans to boil up again once before serving.

How to cook beans in the pressure cooker
Cooking time: 45 minutes

This method considerably reduces the cooking time and the result is almost as flavoursome as after lengthy cooking.

500 g (1 lb 2 oz) beans	2 tablespoons lard
2 onions	Salt
2 cloves garlic	

Pick over and wash the beans and soak in boiling water in a covered basin for an hour. Drain the beans, make up the soaking water to 1 litre (1¾ pints) and bring to the boil in the open pressure cooker. Add the soaked beans, onions and garlic, bring to the boil and skim. Reduce the heat so that the contents are simmering but not rising in the pan. Place the lid on the pressure cooker and bring to 7 kilo (15¾ lb) or high pressure point. Cook thus for 20 minutes, then reduce pressure, add the lard and salt and bring up to pressure slowly once more for 10 minutes. Reduce pressure at room temperature and serve.

Refritos
Mashed Beans

An alternative way to eat beans after the main meat course, with fried eggs for breakfast or in *tortas*, *tacos* or *gorditas*.

500 g (1 *lb* 2 *oz*) *cooked beans*
   and their cooking liquor
4 *tablespoons lard*

100 g (4 *oz*) *grated cheese*
4 *tortillas*

Drain the broth from the beans and mash them with a wooden spoon or potato masher. Sauté the mashed beans in 2 tablespoons of lard, adding a cup of broth. Allow to simmer until it thickens into a heavy paste which can be rolled up. Serve hot, rolled up and garnished with grated cheese and triangles of tortilla fried in the rest of the lard.

Chile con Carne
Chile and Meat

Chile con carne is strictly speaking not a Mexican dish but rather one of North American origin. However, as it is so well known and a delicious way of combining meat and beans, it deserves to be included.

150 g (5½ *oz*) *kidney beans*
500 g (1 *lb* 2 *oz*) *minced pork*
350 g (12 *oz*) *minced veal or*
   beef
5 *small red chiles*
1 *onion*
2 *cloves garlic*

½ *teaspoon oregano*
5 *cumin seeds*
2 *cups tomato purée* (*p.* 18)
2 *tablespoons flour*
2 *tablespoons lard*
Salt

Soak the beans overnight and boil with a clove of garlic and a piece of onion, adding a knob of lard after 2 hours and salt 10 minutes before they are ready. Or, more simply, open a tin of red kidney beans!

In a separate pan, cook the meat in ½ litre (1 pint) of water and salt to taste for 30 minutes. Clean the chiles and soak them in hot water for 30 minutes. Grind them with the onion, garlic, oregano and cumin seeds and add a little of the water in which they soaked and the tomato purée. Brown the flour in the lard and add the chile and tomato mixture, the cooked, minced meats and a cup of the meat stock. Cover the casserole and leave to simmer until the sauce has thickened. Add the cooked beans and the juice which has exuded from them. Season with salt. Simmer for 10 minutes and serve with Mexican white rice and/or tortillas.

Frijol Blanco con Puerco
Pork and Beans

Pork and beans team up well together especially in this recipe from Puebla.

250 g (9 oz) haricot beans	1 chorizo (see p. 17)
50 g (2 oz) bacon	50 g (2 oz) ham
500 g (1 lb 2 oz) pork loin or belly	100 g (4 oz) white cabbage
300 g (10 oz) tomatoes	1 teaspoon turmeric
2 onions	2 cloves
	Salt and pepper

Soak the beans overnight in cold water. Place to boil in plenty of water with the diced bacon for 3 hours (or for 20 minutes with 1 litre/1¾ pints water in the pressure cooker). Boil the pork for 1½ hours or until well cooked. Purée the tomatoes and onions. Dice the pork, chorizo, and ham and add to the tender beans with the tomato and onion purée, the shredded cabbage, turmeric, cloves, salt and pepper. Leave to simmer a further 15–30 minutes until the cabbage is tender and the flavours have mingled. Serve immediately with tortillas and Mexican white rice.

Rollo de Frijoles
Bean Roll

A delicious accompaniment to a plain meat or fish dish or savoury pie. Double the quantities for a supper dish for 6.

250 g (9 oz) tomatoes	100 g (4 oz) grated cheese
1 onion	1 avocado
4 tablespoons lard	2 tortillas
500 g (1 lb 2 oz) cooked pink	1 bunch radishes
beans	2 pickled chipotle chiles
1 tin sardines	

Toast the tomatoes and purée with the onion. Sauté in 2 tablespoons of lard until it thickens. Add the mashed beans and when the mixture begins to thicken, add the minced sardines. When this is dry, roll up the mixture, garnish with grated cheese, avocado strips, triangles of fried tortillas, radishes and strips of chile.

Mitos
Sardine Bean Patties

Use up left-over beans to make this tasty supper dish.

500 g (1 lb 2 oz) cooked beans	3 eggs
and their cooking liquor	½ litre (1 pint) tomato purée
4 onions	(p. 18)
Lard or oil for frying	1 teaspoon chile powder
2 tins sardines in tomato	2 tablespoons chopped
sauce	parsley
6 tablespoons flour	

Mash the beans with a little of their broth and fry with 2 chopped onions in 4 tablespoons of oil until they form a paste. Remove the paste from the heat and allow to cool. Roll out the paste and cut into small rectangles, filling each with a sardine and rolling it up, the size of a small sausage roll. Dip the rolls in the flour and in beaten egg and fry. Serve hot smothered in sauce and sprinkled with chopped parsley. Accompany with tortillas and/or Mexican white rice and a green salad.

To make the sauce: Sauté a chopped onion, the tomato

purée and chile powder in 2 tablespoons of lard. Season with salt and allow to simmer till thickened.

Bandera de Frijoles
Mexican Flag Pie

This dish takes its name from the green, white and red garnishes, the colours of the Mexican flag.

1 kg (2¼ lb) cooked pink beans	500 g (1 lb 2 oz) cooked pork loin
2 cloves garlic	2 tablespoons lard
⅛ litre (¼ pint) oil	1 teaspoon chile powder
1 tablespoon flour	½ teaspoon oregano
500 g (1 lb 2 oz) tomatoes	Salt and pepper
1 onion	

For garnish:

2 avocados	2 red peppers
50 g (2 oz) white cheddar	

Mash the beans. Brown the garlic in the oil, remove and fry the flour. When it is brown, add the cooked, mashed beans, stirring well. Purée the tomatoes and onion. Dice the cooked pork and sauté in lard. Add the purée, chile powder, oregano, salt and pepper and leave to simmer till thick.

Grease a rectangular baking dish. Spread half the mashed beans over the bottom, then put in a layer of meat and top with the rest of the bean mixture. Bake for 30 minutes in a moderate oven until the edges shrink from the sides of the pan. Turn out on to a large platter and garnish with the mashed avocado, grated cheese and red peppers in 3 broad stripes to form the Mexican flag. Serve with Mexican white rice with a mixed salad to follow.

See also **Chiles rellenos de frijoles** (p. 90).

Maize

Maize forms the basis of many tasty dishes, either as corn kernels, tortillas or fresh cornmeal dough.

DISHES MADE WITH TORTILLAS

Enchiladas
Enchiladas

Justifiably one of Mexico's most celebrated dishes – tortillas are wrapped round a meat filling, then smothered in a mole-type sauce.

Enchiladas Rojas
Red Enchiladas

24 *tortillas*
250 g (9 oz) *lard*

For the filling:
250 g (9 oz) *cooked chicken, turkey or beef or 2 chorizos or ordinary pork sausage*

For the sauce:
10 *ancho chiles*
1 *large tablespoon sugar*
1 *large bar plain chocolate*
1 *stick cinnamon*
1 *slice stale bread*

Salt to taste
¼ *litre (½ pint) hot water or stock*
250 g (9 oz) *parmesan cheese*
1 *large onion*

Toast and clean the chiles, soak them in hot water. When the chile is well soaked, grind together with the sugar, chocolate, cinnamon, bread and a little salt. Add hot water or stock and allow to simmer till the sauce is thick.

Meanwhile, fry the tortillas in hot lard, place some filling on each tortilla and roll it up. Place 4 or 5 rolled-up tortillas on each plate, cover with the sauce and garnish with finely chopped onion and grated cheese.

Enchiladas Verdes
Green Enchiladas

This dish is difficult to reproduce without Mexican green tomatoes but a fair approximation can be made by choosing very firm, greenish ordinary tomatoes.

250 g (9 oz) pork loin	1 cup lard
8 poblano chiles	50 g (2 oz) cream cheese
100 g (4 oz) Mexican green tomatoes (see p. 18)	2 onions
	Salt and pepper
1 egg	50 g (2 oz) Cheshire cheese
¼ litre (½ pint) single cream	1 lettuce
24 tortillas	12 radishes

Boil the pork in a little water until tender. Toast and clean the chiles and grind them with the boiled tomatoes. Beat the egg with the cream and add to the tomato and chile mixture. Dip the tortillas in this mixture and brown them in hot fat. Place some filling on each tortilla, roll it up and serve hot, sprinkled with fresh crumbled cheese and garnished with lettuce leaves and radishes.

For the filling: Shred the well-cooked pork and mix with the cream cheese and finely chopped onion. Add salt and pepper to taste.

Panuchos
Panuchos

These are a delicious Yucatecan snack, served with an extremely piquant chile sauce.

500 g (1 *lb* 2 *oz*) *black beans* (*boiled and mashed, see p*. 15)	1 *onion*
	30 *tortillas*
	2 *cups lard*
6 *serrano chiles*	2 *chicken breasts*

For the sauce:

4 *large onions*	10 *cumin seeds*
1 *cup vinegar*	5 *cloves garlic* (*toasted*)
4 *habanera chiles*	½ *teaspoon oregano*
12 *peppercorns*	2 *bay leaves*

After mashing the beans, re-fry them with the chiles and chopped onion.

Carefully lift the delicate skin on top of the tortilla. Fill the tortillas with the bean mixture. When ready to serve, fry the filled tortillas, drain and top with some cooked, shredded chicken. Hand round a bowl of sauce made as follows:

Chop the onions, soak briefly in salted water, drain and boil with the vinegar, the chiles, spices and herbs. Allow to boil up once, then serve.

Enrollados
Enrollados

Tortillas wrapped round a meat, onion, potato and tomato filling in a hot sauce.

250 g (9 *oz*) *pork loin*	*Salt and pepper*
250 g (9 *oz*) *potatoes*	12 *tortillas*
1 *small cup lard*	4 *tablespoons flour*
1 *onion*	3 *eggs*
¼ *litre* (½ *pint*) *tomato purée*	

M.C.T.—6

For the sauce:

1 *onion*	*Salt and pepper*
1 *tablespoon lard*	1 *sprig coriander leaf*
3 *serrano chiles*	2 *avocados*
¼ *litre (½ pint) tomato purée* (*p.* 18)	

To garnish:

1 *onion*	1 *lettuce*
12 *small radishes*	50 *g (2 oz) grated cheese*

Boil the pork till well cooked through and shred the meat. Boil the potatoes and slice. Sauté them in a tablespoon of lard along with the chopped onion and the tomato purée. Season with salt and pepper and simmer till thick. Place some of the mixture on each tortilla; roll up the tortilla, dip in flour and then in the beaten eggs and fry in good hot fat.

Meanwhile, make the sauce: Brown a chopped onion in 1 tablespoon of lard, adding the toasted de-veined chiles and finally the tomato purée. Season with salt and pepper and leave to simmer until thick. Remove the sauce from the heat and add the chopped coriander leaf and sliced avocados. Pour the sauce over the hot fried tortillas and serve garnished with slices of onion, radishes and lettuce, sprinkled with grated cheese.

DISHES MADE WITH CORNMEAL FLOUR

Chalupas
Chalupas (Narrow-boats)

A dish from Puebla in which tortillas are topped with a spicy meat mixture in a green tomato and chile sauce.

500 g (1 lb 2 oz) cornmeal
   dough (made from Minza
   or Quaker Masa Harina)
150 g (5½ oz) lard

4 onions
250 g (9 oz) cooked,
   shredded pork loin

For the Green Sauce:

20 Mexican green tomatoes
2 tablespoons coriander leaf

2 serrano chiles
1 clove garlic

Add a little extra water to the cornmeal dough (see p. 12) to make it light and smooth. Knead, shape into tortillas and bake on a hot plate or ungreased frying-pan, turning up the edges slightly. Place all the tortillas on a large baking-tray on the hot plate. Place on each tortilla a little burnt lard, some green sauce, some finely chopped onion, the shredded, cooked pork and a little more lard. Serve piping hot.

To make the sauce: Boil the tomatoes for 30 minutes in a little water. If they are tinned, boil for 15 minutes in their own juice. Grind them with the chiles, garlic and coriander leaf. Pour into a saucepan and simmer for 10 minutes with 1 tablespoon of lard. The sauce is then ready to spoon over the tortillas.

Dedos de Charro
Rancher's Fingers

Special tortillas wrapped round a pork, chile and chocolate filling smothered in cream and browned in the oven.

250 g (9 oz) cornmeal dough
   (made from Minza or
   Quaker Masa Harina)
100 g (4 oz) flour
1 egg
1 teaspoon salt

1 teaspoon baking powder
200 g (7 oz) lard
1 egg white
¼ litre (½ pint) single cream
100 g (4 oz) Cheshire cheese
50 g (2 oz) butter

Filling

250 g (9 oz) pork loin	2 mulato red chiles
30g (1 oz) bread	50 g (2 oz) lard
1 tortilla	30 g (1 oz) chocolate
3 tablespoons sesame seeds	1 onion
2 pasilla red chiles	½ litre (¼ pint) pork stock
2 ancho red chiles	Salt and pepper to taste

Cook the pork in boiling water. Meanwhile, knead together the cornmeal dough, flour, egg, salt and baking powder with 1 tablespoon lard. Roll out the dough to ½ cm (¼ in) thick and cut off rectangular strips 12×5 cm (5×2 in). Place a little of the filling along the rectangle and roll it up like a sausage roll, sealing the edge with egg white. Fry in lard till golden brown, then place in a baking dish. Pour over the cream, crumble the cheese over the top and dot with butter. Place in a moderate oven for 30 minutes to brown.

To make the filling: Fry the bread, tortillas, sesame seeds and peeled, de-veined chiles in half the lard. Add the chocolate and grind with the onion in the stock. Dice the well-cooked pork and allow to simmer in the chile sauce with salt and pepper to taste, until thickened.

Quesadillas
Quesadillas

A favourite snack, tortillas with a delicious cheesy filling, deep fried and garnished with onions and avocado strips. In some regions of Mexico, there are special quesadilla stalls: the tortillas are wrapped tightly round a long cylinder of cheese cut with an apple corer before being deep-fried. You may wish to try these with a chile and tomato sauce or you may prefer the cresent-shaped quesadillas with a more spicy filling as given here.

6 ancho chiles	1 kg (2¼ lb) fresh cornmeal dough (made from Minza or Quaker Masa Harina)

Salt

1 cup lard

1 bunch spring onions

3 avocados

Filling

3 cloves garlic

500 g (1 lb 2 oz) tomatoes

12 green chiles

1 tablespoon lard

Salt

500 g (1 lb 2 oz) cheese

Clean the ancho chiles and soak for an hour in cold water. Drain well and grind with the cornmeal dough which has been allowed to dry out a little. Mix well, adding salt and if the dough seems too moist, add a little flour. Shape into tortillas (see p. 14). When baking them on a hot plate or ungreased frying-pan, place a little filling in the centre of each and fold it over, pressing firmly round the edge. Bake on the griddle until the dough blisters.

Place the hot quesadillas in a deep pot and cover so that they do not harden. When ready to serve, brown lightly in hot lard and garnish with the onions and avocado strips.

For the filling: Chop the garlic, tomatoes and small green chiles. Sauté in 1 tablespoon lard, season with salt and leave to simmer until thick. Leave the mixture to cool, then mix with the grated cheese.

Sopes
Sopes

Another very tasty tortilla snack, popular in Mexico City. This time, two tortillas are sandwiched together round a cheese, tomato and bean filling, deep fried and garnished with lettuce, avocado, chorizo sausage and radishes.

3 ancho chiles

250 g (9 oz) fresh cornmeal
  dough (made from Minza
  or Quaker Masa Harina)

4 tablespoons flour

1 egg and 1 egg white

150 g (5½ oz) lard

Salt

Filling

150 g (5½ oz) pink or black beans	1 onion
	Salt
50 g (2 oz) lard	50 g (2 oz) grated cheese
250 g (9 oz) tomatoes	

Garnish

1 lettuce	2 avocados
100 g (4 oz) grated cheese	1 bunch radishes
2 chorizos or ordinary pork sausages (optional)	Salt, pepper and Tabasco sauce to taste

Clean and soak the chiles and grind and mix with the corn-meal dough. Add the flour, the whole egg, 1 teaspoon of lard and the salt. Mix well. Shape tortillas with this mixture (see p. 14).

To make the filling: Boil the beans as usual (see p. 15). When they are tender, mash and sauté in lard with the boiled, peeled and sieved tomatoes, the finely chopped onion and a little salt. Mix in the cheese. Place a layer of the filling between two tortillas, seal the edges with egg white and fry in very hot lard.

Serve the *sopes* with a topping of shredded lettuce, grated cheese, fried chorizo sausage, sliced avocado, radish and a few drops of Tabasco sauce.

Gorditas
Gorditas

Gorditas or *fatties* are thick potato and cornmeal dough tortillas topped with shredded pork and guacamole sauce. These are often sold at roadside stalls as a substantial snack for weary travellers.

250 g (9 oz) potatoes
250 g (9 oz) fresh cornmeal
   dough (made from Minza
   or Quaker Masa Harina)
100 g (4 oz) flour

1 egg
50 g (2 oz) grated cheese
225 g (8 oz) lard
150 g (6 oz) cooked pork

Boil and mash the potatoes. Mix with the dough, the flour, the egg, the grated cheese, 1 tablespoon of lard and salt. Form into round rissole shapes and fry in very hot fat. Serve at once, topped with the shredded pork and some guacamole sauce (see p. 129).

Chilaquiles
Chilaquiles

Made from tortillas left over from the day before, this dish is hailed in Mexico as an excellent antidote for a hangover and is served at breakfast time. You may find it more appropriate as a light supper-dish in Britain, resembling in texture and flavour a layered pasta dish.

25 stale tortillas
1 cup lard
500 g (1 lb 2 oz) Mexican
   green tomatoes (see p. 18)
3 serrano chiles
3 sprigs coriander leaf

2 onions
100 g (4 oz) grated cheese
1 cup meat stock
2 hard-boiled eggs
1 bunch radishes

Cut up the tortillas and fry in the lard but do not brown. Drain. Boil the tomatoes and grind them with the chiles, coriander leaf and onion and then sauté in a little lard. In a large flat-bottomed casserole place a layer of fried tortilla, a layer of grated cheese, a layer of sauce and top with more tortilla. Pour over the remaining sauce and the meat stock. Cook over a low flame so that the tortilla is softened but not dried. Remove from the heat. Sprinkle each serving with grated cheese, chopped coriander, chopped onion and garnish with slices of hard-boiled egg and radish.

Tamales
Tamales

Tamales, little patties made from corn kernels or from tortilla dough with a spicy savoury or a sweet filling are a great favourite for fiestas. In most Mexican towns you will find a lady selling them hot from a deep earthenware pot in the *zocalo* or main square. They are usually accompanied with a mug of steaming hot *atole* (see p. 156). Here is a recipe for savoury tamales especially adapted for the British kitchen.

300 g (11 oz) lard
500 g (1 lb 2 oz) tortilla flour
   (Minza or Quaker Masa
   Harina)
100 g (4 oz) rice flour
1 cup chicken stock

1 tablespoon baking powder
Salt
12 leaves from corn on the
   cob or 12 small pieces of
   muslin, cut 10 × 20 cm
   (4 × 8 in) and folded in half

For the filling:
1 onion
3 tablespoons lard
2 tablespoons chile powder
2 tablespoons flour
⅛ litre (¼ pint) chicken stock
1½ cups tomato sauce (made
   from 675 g/1½ lb tomatoes
   simmered with 1 onion and
   2 cloves garlic, seasoned
   with salt and pepper)

½ teaspoon ground cinnamon
½ teaspoon ground cloves
Salt and pepper to taste
1 chicken

Cream the lard. Bit by bit, add the tortilla flour, rice flour, stock, baking powder and salt. Beat until a little of the batter will float in a glass of water. Put a tablespoonful of the mixture on the cob leaf or piece of muslin. Make a small well in the centre of the dough and place some filling in it, folding the wrapping over it. Place the wrapped up tamales in the top of a steamer, leaving a space in the centre. Place a napkin on top and then the lid. Leave to steam for an hour, then serve piping hot.

To make the filling: Sauté the onion in the lard. Mix the chile powder with the flour and chicken stock and add to the onion until it begins to thicken. Add the tomato sauce, spices, salt, pepper and cooked chicken meat. Leave to simmer until thick.

Tamales Dulces
Sweet Tamales

250 g (9 oz) lard
200 g (7 oz) sugar
450 g (1 lb) tortilla flour
100 g (4 oz) rice flour
1 tablespoon baking powder
½ teaspoon salt
¼ litre (½ pint) stock

50 g (2 oz) raisins
50 g (2 oz) almonds
50 g (2 oz) candied citron
Leaves from corn on the cob
  or pieces of muslin cut
  10 × 20 cm (8 × 16 in) and
  folded in half

Cream the lard with the sugar until fluffy. Bit by bit, add the tortilla flour, rice flour, baking powder, salt and stock. Continue beating until a little dough will float in a glass of water. Place a tablespoonful of dough on each moistened leaf or piece of muslin. In a well in the centre, add the raisins, slivers of almond and candied citron. Wrap and steam as in the previous recipe until the tamales have shrunk from their wrapping. Serve immediately.

RECIPES FROM MAIZE KERNELS

Pozole
Pozole

A warm and nourishing soup-stew.

250 g (9 oz) very coarse grains of maize	250 g (9 oz) pork loin
3 tablespoons lime (calcium hydroxide, or slaked lime, available at your chemist)	1 chicken
	Salt
	4 large onions
1 clove garlic	1 bunch radishes
250 g (9 oz) pig's head	5 lemons
1 pair pig's trotters	1 small bowlful oregano

Wash the maize and boil with the lime in 2 litres (3½ pints) water until the skins loosen. Rinse and remove the skins by rubbing the kernels together briskly. Remove the tips. Boil the maize with the garlic until the kernels soften. Cut up the pork and chicken and continue cooking slowly until all are well cooked, adding salt and more water as required. Serve the soup-stew garnished with finely chopped onion, radishes, wedges of lemon to squeeze over it and a lavish sprinkling of oregano.

Budín de Elote
Corn Pudding

A delicious creamy vegetable accompaniment to a main meat dish.

6 corns on the cob or 2 tins corn kernels	1 tablespoon sugar
	1 cup milk
150 g (5½ oz) butter	3 tablespoons breadcrumbs
6 eggs	½ cup double cream
1 teaspoon salt	

Scrape the kernels from the corn cobs or empty and drain the tin of sweet corn. Grind the kernels. Cream the butter. Add, mixing well, the ground corn, the whole eggs one at a time, the salt, sugar and milk. Pour the mixture into a ring mould, greased and lined with breadcrumbs. Bake in a moderate oven for 45 minutes or until the eggs have set. Invert the pudding on to a platter and fill the centre of the ring with the stiffly beaten cream, seasoned with salt and pepper. Serve hot with fried meat and Mexican white rice.

Snacks

The Mexicans have a simply vast number of savoury snacks which are made up at home or can be bought at *tacerías* or *torterías*. These are small restaurants or shops either outside or indoors where snacks are made and sold – in fact, at Xochimilco, where a marvellous day out can be had listening to mariachi bands whilst being punted along the canals between the floating gardens on flower-covered barges, several ladies cook on board and come alongside to sell their *tacos*. Usually they are kiosks simply laden with dishes of different meats, chiles, sauces and beans. You ask for a tortilla or torta roll to be filled with whatever you fancy. A tortilla round meat and sauce or with a vegetable or cheese filling is a *taco*. A warm bread-roll sandwich is a *torta*.

Tacos
Tacos

My favourite *taco* is chopped fried steak with *salsa roja* (see p. 128) or *guacamole* (see p. 129) and a few beans rolled into a fresh hot tortilla. (You will probably want 3 or 4 at a sitting.) But any cooked meat – chicken, pork, etc. – is quite delicious.

Tortas
Tortas

Torta rolls are large and flattish and have nice crusty outsides a little softer than French bread. An English dinner roll or something slightly larger if available would be a suitable substitute. Tortas, too, can have a wide variety of fillings which you can combine to taste.

Fresh rolls
Roast meat (chicken, leg of pork, beef, veal, chorizo, etc.)
Mayonnaise
Beans refritos (see p. 102)
Chopped tomato

Chopped onion
Whole pickled chiles (see p. 127)
Avocado
Chopped coriander leaf
Salt and pepper

A large hot plate is ideal for making tortas but 2 large frying-pans will serve.

First, slice the rolls in half, remove some of the soft dough from the centre and put the rolls to heat on both sides on the hot plate. Also place the chopped meat on the hot plate or griddle. When both are heated through, take up the halves of roll, spread some mayonnaise over them, add a thin layer of the mashed beans, the meat, a sprinkling of chopped tomato and chopped onion, one whole chile and a slice of avocado. Add a little coriander leaf, salt and pepper and squash down the top of the roll.

Tortas are usually washed down with a *licuado* (fresh fruit juice – see p. 157) or a beer with salt and lemon sprinkled on top.

Eggs

Huevos Rancheros
Rancher's Eggs

A favourite breakfast dish, possibly better suited to the British palate as a light supper dish or brunch.

6 tortillas
150 g (5½ oz) lard
6 eggs
100 g (4 oz) cheese
2 avocados

1 onion
1 clove garlic
Green chiles to taste (½ to 2)
250 g (9 oz) tomatoes
Salt

Fry each tortilla in lard but do not brown. Fry the eggs. Place each egg carefully on a tortilla, pour some sauce over each and garnish with cheese and avocado. Serve immediately.

To make the sauce: Chop the onion finely with the garlic and chile and the boiled, peeled, sieved tomatoes and sauté in a little lard. Add salt to taste and leave to simmer until fairly thick and the eggs are ready.

Huevos Revueltos
Scrambled Eggs

Like British scrambled eggs with the addition of chile, tomato and onion. The Mexicans do not add milk or butter to the eggs, the consistency thus being rather harder than its British equivalent.

1 small onion
1 clove garlic
Green chiles to taste
2 tablespoons lard

100 g (4 oz) tomatoes
Salt and pepper
6 eggs

Chop the onion, garlic and chile and sauté in lard. Add the tomatoes and salt to taste. Leave to simmer for a few minutes, then add the lightly beaten eggs. Scramble and serve as soon as the eggs are firm.

Huevos en Rabo de Mestiza
Hard-boiled Eggs in a Hot Sauce

A quick and tasty meal: just the job for an unexpected vegetarian guest.

3 *poblano chiles*	1½ *cups milk*
2 *tablespoons lard*	½ *cup cream*
1 *small onion*	150 g (5½ oz) *cheese*
6 *tomatoes* (*puréed*)	6 *hard-boiled eggs*
Salt and pepper	

Toast the chiles, remove veins and seeds and cut into strips. Sauté in the lard, then add the finely chopped onion and when it is golden brown, add the puréed tomatoes. Add salt and pepper to taste and simmer for 10 minutes. Add the milk, cream and grated cheese and leave to simmer on a very low light until the mixture thickens.

Slice the hard-boiled eggs and add to the mixture. Leave to simmer for about 5 minutes longer and serve piping hot with Mexican white rice.

Huevos Tricolor
Mexican Flag Eggs

3 *tablespoons chopped parsley*	*Salt and pepper*
6 *eggs*	6 *slices of tomato*
25 g (1 oz) *butter*	*Oil and vinegar to taste*

Butter 6 individual moulds. Sprinkle with chopped parsley. Empty a raw egg into each mould, taking care not to break the yolk. Put a dot of butter and some salt and pepper on top of the egg. Place the moulds in a *bain marie* with very little water so that it does not splash into the moulds. Cook for 5–10 minutes, then turn each egg out on to a slice of tomato seasoned with oil and vinegar. Serve cold. If you wish to serve the eggs hot, turn them out on to pieces of bread and cover them with a thick tomato sauce.

Huevos Elena
Eggs Elena

A delicious egg and vegetable dish.

1 *small onion*	3 *cooked, chopped carrots*
Butter	12 *eggs*
150 g (5½ oz) *ham*	*Salt and pepper*
1 *cup cooked peas*	*White sauce*
1 *cup cooked, chopped green beans*	

Fry the onion in butter. When it is golden brown, add the chopped ham, then the chopped vegetables.

Butter 6 large individual moulds and fill the bottom with vegetables to just over half way. Beat the eggs and pour an equal amount into each mould. Add salt and pepper and a dot of butter. Place in a moderate oven in a *bain marie* for 30 minutes or until the egg has set. Turn out on to a plate and pour a white sauce over the egg-and-vegetable moulds.

Niditos de Arroz
Little Rice Nests

Bacon and eggs with a difference – an attractive light supper or lunch dish.

1½ *cups cooked rice*	6 *eggs*
6 *tablespoons milk*	25 g (1 oz) *butter*
6 *rashers bacon*	*Salt and pepper to taste*

Cook the rice in salted water. Drain well and add the milk to bind the rice together. Fry the bacon rashers and remove from the fat when they are just cooked. On a well-greased baking-tray, form 6 little nests with the rice and place a piece of bacon round each secured with a tooth-pick. Empty a raw egg into the well in the centre of the rice, top with a dot of butter, season to taste and place in a moderate oven for 5 or 10 minutes until the white of the egg is firm but the yolk soft.

Huevos Exquisitos
Exquisite Eggs

Eggs on a bed of tortilla and beans with a tomato, chile and onion sauce.

100 g (4 oz) cooked beans and
    their cooking liquid
6 tablespoons lard
1 onion
2 poblano chiles or green
    peppers

1 cup tomato purée (p. 18)
6 tortillas
6 eggs
2 tablespoons grated cheese

Mash the beans and fry in lard with some of their stock, until they form a paste.

Make a sauce by chopping the onion and sautéing it in lard with the toasted, cleaned and sliced chiles. Add the tomato purée and allow to simmer until thick.

Fry the tortillas in lard and drain. Fry the eggs. On each tortilla, place a layer of beans and one egg. Cover with sauce, sprinkle with grated cheese and serve immediately.

Tortilla de Huevos a la Mexicana
Mexican Omelette

6 *eggs*	1 *onion*
Salt and pepper to taste	*Lard*
1 *tablespoon chopped parsley*	250 *g (9 oz) cooked potatoes*
1 *dessertspoonful flour*	

Beat the eggs with a little salt and pepper, the parsley and 1 dessertspoonful of flour. Fry the finely chopped onion till golden brown, then add the cooked potatoes chopped in fingers. When these are golden brown, pour the eggs on top and leave to fry a little. Turn the omelette out on to a large plate. Add a little more oil to the frying-pan and carefully slide the omelette back in to cook the other side. Use a low light so that the omelette does not burn before the middle is cooked.

There are many variations on this theme, adding pieces of chorizo, ham, bacon and any left-over vegetables.

Tortilla de Huevos con Camarones
Shrimp Omelette

A simple dish transformed.

250 *g (9 oz) fresh shrimps*	*Salt and pepper to taste*
6 *eggs*	2 *tablespoons butter or oil*
4 *tablespoons milk*	100 *g (4 oz) flaked almonds*

Cook the shrimps, peel and clean them thoroughly. Chop up half and reserve half to garnish the omelette. Beat the eggs, mix in the milk and add salt and pepper. Melt 2 tablespoons of butter in a large frying-pan. When it is very hot, pour in the eggs and cook on a low heat. When the bottom is cooked but the top is still soft, add the chopped shrimps and half the almonds. Roll up the omelette and serve immediately sprinkled with the rest of the almonds and surrounded by the whole shrimps.

Sauces

The different chile sauces which always accompany Mexican dishes and salads are as indispensable as the tortilla and the bean. Luckily, it is possible to find the ingredients for the most common sauces which I include here at most greengrocers or delicatessens in Britain. Tabasco sauce can be bought anywhere and is delicious sprinkled over *huevos estrellados* (fried eggs) with beans and tortillas but it does not take a moment to make up a fresh sauce and it has a crunchy quality which the bottled variety lacks.

Chiles en Vinagre
Pickled Chiles

A very useful standby especially if chiles are not often available at your local greengrocer. They can be chopped up in chile sauces or in stews and can be eaten whole in *tortas*, to accompany meat dishes and cold platters. The Mexicans usually make a mixed pickle as in the recipe which follows.

500 g (1 *lb* 2 *oz*) small green
  chiles
2 *medium-sized carrots*

½ *small firm cauliflower*
6 *cloves garlic*

For the brine:
1 *litre* (1¾ *pints*) *water*
100 g (4 *oz*) *salt*

For the spiced vinegar:
1 *litre* (1¾ *pints*) *vinegar*
2 *sticks cinnamon*
4 *teaspoons cloves*

4 *teaspoons whole mace*
4 *teaspoons allspice*
A few peppercorns

Toast the chiles well all over under the grill. Peel off the skins. Peel and wash the carrots and cut into thin rounds.

Break off small flowerets of cauliflower. Peel the cloves of garlic. Mix all the vegetables together in a bowl. Add the brine and leave to steep overnight, keeping the vegetables immersed as much as possible by placing a plate on top of them.

Meanwhile, prepare the spiced vinegar. Pour the vinegar into a basin containing the cinnamon, cloves, mace, allspice and peppercorns. Stand the basin in a saucepan of water. The bowl containing the vinegar should be covered so that the flavour does not escape. Bring the water to the boil, then remove from the heat. Leave the spices to steep in the vinegar for 2 hours, then strain. The following day, remove the vegetables from the brine and rinse in cold water. Drain thoroughly. Arrange the chiles, pieces of cauliflower, carrot and garlic neatly in jars without packing them too tightly. Pour the vinegar over the vegetables and seal. A disc of ceresin paper in the lid will prevent corrosion of the lid (if it is metal) and evaporation of the vinegar.

Salsa Roja
Red Sauce

Most cafés in Mexico have bowls of *salsa roja* on the table along with the salt and pepper and, indeed, it is eaten most commonly in every family with meat, beans and tortillas, in tacos, etc.

1 *clove garlic*
3 *or* 4 *small green chiles*
1 *onion*
4 *large tomatoes*

1 *tablespoon chopped*
  coriander leaf
Salt and pepper

Grind the garlic, along with the de-seeded, chopped chiles. Chop the onion finely and add the chopped tomato, coriander leaf and ground garlic and chile. Add salt and pepper to taste. Mix well and serve.

Guacamole
Guacamole

Usually a choice of sauce is offered, especially where tacos are concerned. The other sauce is generally the avocado-based *guacamole* often scooped up on pieces of *chicharrón* (see p. 17).

2 *ripe avocados (large)*
2 *tomatoes*
1 *small green chile*
1 *bunch spring onions*
A squeeze of lemon juice

1 *tablespoon chopped coriander leaf or a pinch of oregano*
Salt

Mash the pulp of the avocados. Grind the skinned tomatoes with the de-seeded chopped chile. Chop the onions very fine and mix all the ingredients together with the lemon juice, coriander leaf (or oregano) and salt to taste.

Salsa para Lechuga
Salad Dressing

A slight variation on the French version with the addition of mint and the use of lemon juice in place of vinegar.

For 1 lettuce:
2 *large cloves garlic*
2 *mint leaves*
2 *tablespoons lemon juice*
4 *tablespoons olive oil*

1 *teaspoon sugar*
A little freshly ground pepper
Salt

Crush the cloves of garlic, toast the mint leaves and leave them to soak in the lemon juice for 2 hours before preparing the salad. Remove the garlic and mint from the lemon juice and mix the oil with the flavoured juice. Mix in the sugar, pepper and salt to taste. Pour the dressing over the previously washed, well-dried, shredded lettuce, toss and serve.

Salsa Verde Poblana
Pueblan Green Sauce

This sauce from the town of Puebla is particularly good served with *enchiladas* and to accompany meat dishes.

10 *large poblano chiles*	¼ *litre* (½ *pint*) *fresh cream*
1 *large onion*	*Salt*
5 *small green chiles*	100 *g* (4 *oz*) *parmesan*
50 *g* (2 *oz*) *butter*	

Wash, toast, peel and seed the poblano chiles (if they are tinned, this will have been done for you) and grind with the onion. Fry the small green chiles and pass them through a sieve. Sauté the two types of chile and onion together in butter. When they are heated through, remove from the flame and add the cream, mixing well. Season with salt and sprinkle cheese on top.

Salsa de Semilla de Chile
Chile Seed Sauce

In some regions this strong chile paste is smeared on the *comal* or large earthenware plate on which the tortillas are cooked, giving them a spicy flavour.

3 *tablespoons chile seeds*	*Salt and pepper to taste*
(*ancho, mulato or pasilla*)	1 *finely chopped onion*
6 *tablespoons olive oil*	1 *sprig parsley, finely chopped*
1 *tablespoon lemon juice*	

Wash the chile seeds and brown them in a frying-pan. Grind with a pestle and mortar until a paste is obtained. Add the oil little by little. Put the paste in an earthenware pot and beat until fluffy. Immediately add the lemon juice, salt, pepper, onion and parsley. If it seems very strong, half a teaspoon of sugar may be added.

Mayonesa
Mayonnaise

Mayonnaise is a European import which is greatly appreci-
ated by the Mexicans, who use it often as we would butter
to spread over rolls to make *tortas*, as well as on fish and
salads.

3 *egg yolks*	1 *teaspoon mustard*
1 *cup oil*	*Salt and pepper to taste*
½ *lemon*	

Beat the egg yolks very thoroughly until they thicken. Add
the oil drop by drop beating continually. This is more easily
done by two persons or in a blender because the mayonnaise
may curdle if you stop beating. When all the oil has been
added and the sauce is thick, add the lemon juice in drops,
the salt, pepper and mustard and mix well.

If the mayonnaise should curdle, beat 2 more egg yolks in
a separate bowl until they have thickened; add 3 tablespoons
of oil drop by drop, beating continually, then add little by
little the curdled mayonnaise.

HOT SAUCES

Here are some hot sauces to pour over braised meat.

Salsa de Jitomate
Tomato Sauce

A basic hot chile and tomato sauce which can be used to
liven up any meat or poultry.

2 *poblano chiles*	1 *onion*
1 *tablespoon lard*	4 *tomatoes*
4 *cloves garlic*	*Salt and pepper*

Toast, skin and de-vein the chiles and sauté in lard with the garlic and finely chopped onion. When golden brown, add the tomatoes. Grind or blend all the ingredients, adding salt and pepper to taste. Simmer for a few minutes until the sauce has thickened and the meat is ready to serve.

Salsa de Cebolla
Onion Sauce

A rich, thick sauce to pour over pork, beef or chicken.

2 tablespoons butter	¼ litre (½ pint) milk
2 tablespoons flour	2 egg yolks
1 large onion	Salt and pepper to taste

Melt the butter and add the flour, stirring constantly. Add the finely chopped onion and the milk, little by little, stirring all the time. Leave to simmer for 5 minutes and put in over a *bain marie* for 5 minutes, still stirring. Lastly, pour in the beaten egg yolks. Season with salt and pepper and serve very hot.

Salsa de Ajo
Garlic Sauce

Delicious with white fish, especially salt cod or cod fritters (see p. 49).

2 tablespoons butter	1½ cups milk
2 tablespoons flour	2 eggs
4 whole heads of garlic	Salt and pepper to taste

Melt the butter and brown the flour in it. Add the crushed garlic and the milk little by little, stirring constantly and simmer for 5 minutes. Boil for a further 5 minutes in a *bain marie* and finally stir in the beaten eggs. Season with salt and pepper and serve very hot.

Salsa Agria
Tangy Sauce

This sharp orange and mint-flavoured sauce is particularly good with cold meats (tongue, pork, beef or lamb) or with duck.

½ cup mint leaves
50 g (2 oz) sugar
¼ litre (½ pint) bitter orange
 juice

5 tablespoons vinegar
1 tablespoon orange peel

Chop the mint leaves finely and put to soak with the sugar and orange juice for an hour. Put the vinegar to warm (do not allow to boil) on a low flame. Pour in the mint and orange juice and add the orange peel. An attractive and flavoursome sauce.

Salsa de Almendra Verde
Green Almond Sauce

Delicious with fish, chicken or tongue.

50 g (2 oz) almonds
5 tablespoons chopped parsley
1 clove garlic
3 hard-boiled egg yolks

⅛ litre (⅓ pint) olive oil
3 teaspoons vinegar
Pepper and salt to taste

Put the almonds to soak in boiling water. Peel. Scald the parsley in boiling water. Grind the almonds, parsley, garlic and hard-boiled egg yolk. Add the oil and vinegar and season with salt and pepper.

Salsa Rica
Sumptuous Sauce

A rich and creamy lemon-flavoured sauce which is the perfect accompaniment to any sort of fish.

4 *egg yolks*
3 *tablespoons cold water*
200 *g (7 oz) butter*

1 *tablespoon lemon juice*
Pepper

Put the egg yolks and cold water in a bowl and beat till the water is incorporated. Place the bowl over a pan of hot water and keep beating until it is thick. Add the melted butter, keep beating, add the lemon juice, salt and pepper and beat till thick. Remove from the heat and serve immediately poured over the prepared fish.

Puddings

To end a meal, the Mexican housewife relies very heavily on the glorious abundance of fruit at her disposal, both exotic and tropical fruits such as paw-paws, mangoes, pineapples and *zapotes*, as well as oranges and bananas and fruits from more temperate zones such as apples and pears.

There are, however, several delicious puddings, made from eggs and milk, the most ubiquitous of which is *flan*, crème caramèle. *Flan* is seen everywhere, even on buses in large panniers touted by small boys who jump on and off selling their wares.

Flan a la Antigua
Old-fashioned Crême Caramèle

1 *litre* (1¾ *pints*) *milk*	*A sliver of lemon peel*
200 *g* (7 *oz*) *sugar*	3 *eggs*
1 *stick cinnamon*	6 *egg yolks*

For the caramel:
200 *g* (7 *oz*) *sugar*
8 *tablespoons water*

Boil the milk with the sugar, cinnamon and lemon peel on a low heat for 15 minutes. Strain and leave to cool. Beat the eggs with the yolks and add to the milk. While the milk is cooling, make the caramel by boiling the sugar and water until it turns dark brown. Pour it immediately into a well-greased mould or individual moulds, turning the basin round so that the caramel covers all sides. Pour the milk and egg mixture into the mould and cook in a *bain marie* either on top of the stove or in a moderate oven, until the custard is set (¾–1 hour). Test to see whether it is done by

inserting the blade of a knife into the centre of the custard.
It should come out clean. Cool the custard and turn out on to
a plate to serve.

Flan Normal
Everyday Crême Caramèle

This recipe was given to me by a housewife in Mexico City.
Whilst not being as rich as the Old-fashioned Crême
Caramèle, it is more suitable for everyday occasions, being
quicker to prepare and more economical on egg yolks.

1 *large tin Nestlés milk*	1 *stick cinnamon*
1 *tin water*	1 *sliver of lemon peel*
5 *eggs*	

For the caramel:
100 g (4 *oz*) *sugar*
4 *tablespoons water*

Pour the tin of Nestlés milk into a saucepan with a tin of
water. Bring to the boil with the stick of cinnamon and the
sliver of lemon and allow to simmer on a very low heat for a
few minutes. Meanwhile, make the caramel. Boil the sugar
in the water until a good dark brown colour is obtained.
Butter a mould and pour the caramel into it, turning the
bowl so that it covers all sides. Allow the milk to cool until
you can put your finger into it comfortably, then add the
beaten eggs little by little, stirring all the time. Cook in a
bain marie in a moderate oven for 45 minutes to 1 hour.

Arroz con Leche
Rice Pudding

A great Mexican favourite, this cinnamon-flavoured rice
pudding is delicious hot or cold.

100 g (4 oz) rice
1 stick cinnamon
½ litre (1 pint) water
250 g (9 oz) sugar

1 litre (1¾ pints) milk
2 egg yolks
A small handful of raisins

Soak the rice for 30 minutes in hot water. Rinse and put to boil on a low heat with the stick of cinnamon and the water. When the water has been absorbed, add the sugar and milk and cook until the rice is done. Stir in the beaten egg yolks, add a handful of raisins and serve piping hot or chilled.

Arroz de Leche Tropical
Tropical Rice Pudding

The addition of coconut makes a luscious and doubly nutritious rice pudding.

2 cups shredded or desiccated
    coconut
1 litre (1¾ pints) milk
100 g (4 oz) rice
1 stick cinnamon

½ litre (1 pint) water
250 g (9 oz) sugar
2 egg yolks
30 g (1 oz) raisins

Grind the coconut, dissolve in the milk and strain well. Soak the rice in hot water for 30 minutes. Drain and rinse in cold water. Cook the rice with the cinnamon in the water until the liquid has been absorbed. Add the sugar and the coconut and milk solution. Continue cooking until the rice is tender. Blend in the lightly beaten egg yolks. Boil up once, then pour into serving dishes. Sprinkle with raisins and serve hot or chilled.

Chongos
Chongos

A speciality from Zamora, chongos have a very sweet, rather cheesey flavour. Though the texture can be slightly off-putting for non-aficionados, it is very difficult to resist this tangy dessert once a taste for it is acquired.

2 litres (3½ pints) milk   4 egg yolks
Juice of 2 lemons   1 cup sugar
1 cinnamon stick

Place the milk with the lemon juice in a slightly warm place (e.g. over the pilot light on the stove) to *cortar* (clot). Leave for about 30 minutes. Add the cinnamon and the egg yolks and stir once. Leave for 2 hours. Add the sugar and put on a low heat. Boil gently until the milk is absorbed. DO NOT STIR—only enough to prevent it from sticking. Leave to cool and serve.

Plátanos con Rón
Banana Flambé in Rum

A deliciously simple coastal dish which ends off a meal with a sparkle.

6 bananas   ½ glass rum
75 g (3 oz) butter   ½ litre (1 pint) pouring cream

Slice the bananas lengthwise and cook for a few minutes in the melted butter in a large frying-pan, turning them once. Pour on the rum and as it heats up set light to it. Serve immediately, topped with cream.

Buñuelos de Plátano
Banana Fritters

A delicious way to serve large green bananas.

3 green bananas   2 teaspoons powdered
1 cup olive oil   cinnamon
200 g (7 oz) sugar

Slice the bananas and soak them IN THEIR SKINS for 2 hours in salt water. Drain. Flatten out each slice between the palms of the hands and remove the skin. Fry the slices of banana in oil. Sprinkle with sugar and cinnamon and serve immediately.

Postre Especial
Mexican Trifle

¼ litre (½ pint) water
500 g (1 lb 2 oz) sugar
1 teaspoon ground cinnamon
10 egg yolks
6 tablespoons sweet sherry
¼ litre (½ pint) double cream
3 egg whites

150 g (5½ oz) caster sugar
500 g (1 lb 2 oz) sponge fingers (see p. 142) or trifle sponges
50 g (2 oz) coloured hundreds and thousands

Boil the water with the sugar until a little poured on to a plate forms a thin thread. Remove from the heat, cool and add the cinnamon and lightly beaten egg yolks. Heat over a low light, stirring constantly. When it is thick, remove from the heat and stir in the sherry. Whip the cream. Beat the egg whites with the caster sugar until stiff, and fold into the whipped cream. In a wide-bottomed serving dish, arrange layers of sponge cake, yolk cream and whipped cream, ending with whipped cream and sprinkling the top with hundreds and thousands.

Postre de Yema Entera
Egg Yolk Dessert

A deliciously spicy and rich pudding.

500 g (1 *lb* 2 *oz*) *sugar*
¼ *litre* (½ *pint*) *water*
8 *cloves*
6 *tablespoons sherry*
350 g (12½ *oz*) *sponge fingers*
 (*see p.* 147)

12 *egg yolks*
1 *stick cinnamon*
1 *small handful pine nuts or*
 blanched almonds
1 *small handful raisins*

Boil the sugar with the water and cloves for 5 minutes. Take off the heat and add the sherry. Dip the sponge fingers in the sugar syrup and arrange them round a large plate. Remove the cloves from the rest of the syrup and gradually mix in the egg yolks. Place over a very low light and allow it to thicken, stirring constantly. Pour the custard over the sponge fingers and decorate with the crumbled cinnamon, whole pine nuts or sliced almonds, and raisins.

Torta de Almendras
Almond Torte

A lucious nutty mould.

250 g (9 *oz*) *blanched almonds*
6 *eggs*
A few drops almond essence

300 g (11 *oz*) *sugar*
1 *stick cinnamon*
1 *small handful raisins*

Grind most of the almonds, reserving about 10 for decoration. Separate the eggs and add the yolks gradually to the ground almonds with a few drops of almond essence. Beat the whites till stiff and fork into the almond mixture. Pour into a well-buttered mould dusted with flour and bake in a slow oven for ¾–1 hour. Remove from the oven, slide a knife round the mould and turn out on to a plate. Cover with a syrup made by boiling the sugar and cinnamon in ¼ litre (½ pint) of water for 10 minutes and decorate with flowers made out of toasted halved almonds with a raisin in the centre. Serve cold with whipped or pouring cream.

Postre de Almendra
Almond Trifle

A luxurious almond and sherry trifle.

200 g (7 oz) blanched almonds
500 g (1 lb 2 oz) sugar
¼ litre (½ pint) water

⅛ litre (¼ pint) sweet sherry
6 egg yolks
350 g (12½ oz) sponge fingers (see p. 147)

Grind the almonds. Boil the sugar in the water for 5 minutes. Remove from the heat and pour half of it into a separate pan. Add the sherry to one pan and the ground almonds and lightly beaten egg yolks to the other. Place the almond mixture over a very low heat, stirring constantly until thick. Dip the sponge fingers in the sherry syrup and place in alternate layers with the almond paste in a buttered baking-dish, ending with a layer of almond paste. Bake in a moderate oven until golden brown, about 30 minutes. Serve hot or cold with pouring cream.

Queso de Almendra
Almond Cheese

500 g (1 lb 2 oz) blanched almonds
600 g (1 lb 6 oz) sugar
¼ litre (½ pint) water

8 egg yolks
2 dessertspoons ground cinnamon

Grind the almonds very finely using an electric coffee-mill or blender if available. Boil the sugar with the water for 10 minutes, then remove from the heat and add the ground almonds mixed with the egg yolks. Return the pan to the heat and stir constantly over a very low heat for a few minutes. Remove from the heat and beat into a paste. Grind once more in the blender, then pour the mixture into a round lined tin. Allow to cool, turn out of the tin and remove the greaseproof paper. Sprinkle with plenty of cinnamon and serve in fingers.

Postre de Piña
Pineapple Pudding

A rich pineapple, almond and cinnamon-flavoured custard is poured over sponge fingers.

500 g (1 lb 2 oz) fresh
   pineapple or 2 large tins
   pineapple chunks
150 g (5½ oz) blanched
   almonds
4 egg yolks

250 g (9 oz) sugar
1 stick cinnamon
10 sponge fingers (see p. 147)
25 g (1 oz) raisins
25 g (1 oz) pine nuts

Grind the pineapple in an electric blender and the almonds in a coffee-mill. Beat the egg yolks with the sugar and add the almonds, pineapple and cinnamon. Cook the mixture over a very low heat till the bottom of the pan can be seen. Pour the mixture over the sponge fingers. Decorate with raisins and pine nuts and serve cold with cream.

Cakes, Buns and Biscuits

Pastel de Leche
Plain Cake

A delicious orange-flavoured cake, resembling our Madeira cake.

1 *cup sugar*
5 *eggs*
1 *cup butter*
Peel and juice of 1 *orange*
2½ *cups flour*

3 *teaspoons baking powder*
½ *cup milk*
1 *large handful sultanas*
50 g (2 oz) *almonds*

Beat the sugar with the egg yolks. Add the melted, cooled butter, the grated orange peel and juice. Fold in the flour and baking powder, sifted together. Add the milk, sultanas and almonds and add the egg whites beaten to form peaks. Pour into a greased and floured cake tin and bake in a moderate oven for ¾–1 hour.

Pastel Esponjoso
Sponge Cake

The rising agent here is the egg white, giving a very light sponge.

6 *eggs*
115 g (4 oz) *sugar*

150 g (5½ oz) *flour*
60 g (2 oz) *butter*

Beat the egg yolks with the sugar until lemon-coloured. Add the flour to the yolks bit by bit. Fold in the stiffly beaten egg whites and finally add the melted butter. Pour the mixture into a buttered loaf pan and bake in a moderate oven for 30 minutes. When the cake has risen, quickly make a cut along the top of the cake and return to the oven for a further 10–20 minutes.

Pastel de Pan Frío
Mexican Bread and Butter Cake

Highly recommended, this is a really good way of using up stale bread and you can ring the changes by adding different dried fruits and nuts depending on what you have in the house.

10 *thick slices of stale white bread with a crust*
½ *litre (1 pint) milk*
5 *eggs*
½ *teaspon salt*
1 *cup sugar*
100 g (4 oz) *butter*
A few drops vanilla essence
1 *teaspoon ground cinnamon*

4 *tablespoons brandy or rum*
1–2 *teaspoons baking powder*
100 g (4 oz) *almonds or walnuts*
1 *large handful sultanas*
50 g (2 oz) *cherries*
50 g (2 oz) *figs or dates, finely chopped*

A few hours or the evening before, put the bread to soak in the milk. Make a smooth paste of the milk and bread, with a liquidiser or by hand. Beat the eggs with the salt, sugar, melted butter, vanilla, cinnamon, brandy or rum and the baking powder. Add to the bread and milk paste. If it seems too liquid, add a little flour. When it has a good dropping consistency, add the nuts and fruit, previously chopped and tossed in flour to prevent them sinking. Bake in a moderate oven for about an hour.

Pastel de Nuez
Walnut Cake

500 g (1 *lb* 2 *oz*) *flour*
5 *tablespoons baking powder*
1 *teaspoon salt*
125 g (4½ oz) *butter*

375 g (13 oz) *sugar*
2 *eggs*
150 g (5½ oz) *shelled walnuts*
¼ *litre (½ pint) milk*

Pour the flour in to a flat-bottomed mixing bowl. Make a large well in the centre, sprinkling round it the baking powder and the salt. In the centre, pour the melted butter, sugar, eggs, the broken walnuts and milk. Mix well by hand. Pour into a greased baking-tin and leave to rise for 20 minutes. Then brush with milk or egg and place in a moderate oven for 1 hour or until a knife plunged into the centre of the cake comes out clean.

Rosca de Reyes
Christmas Cake

In most Catholic countries, it is the custom to bake this special cake on the 6th of January when the wise men were supposed to have arrived, bearing gifts, and the children receive their presents. The cake contains a small china doll or a dried bean and the person finding it in his piece of cake must throw a party at his house on the 2nd of February.

450 g (1 lb) flour
15 g (½ oz) dried yeast
115 g (4½ oz) sugar
⅛ litre (¼ pint) warm water
3 whole eggs
Pinch salt
7 egg yolks
2 tablespoons orange blossom water

Grated rind of 1 lemon
200 g (7 oz) butter
2 candied oranges
2 candied citrons
2 tiny china dolls
2 eggs for glaze
100 g (4 oz) caster sugar for sprinkling

Dissolve the yeast in 2 teaspoons sugar and warm water. Add enough flour to form a dough. Shape into a ball and leave in a warm place till it has doubled in size.

Sieve the rest of the flour on to a board, make a well in the centre and add the whole eggs, the granulated sugar and the salt. Knead and then add the egg yolks, orange blossom water, grated lemon rind, the risen dough and the butter in small knobs. Knead thoroughly. Shape into a ball, smear the surface with butter and leave in a warm place for 6 hours.

Knead again and form into a ring on a greased baking tray. Leave to rest in a warm place for 1 hour after inserting the doll into the ring.

Brush with egg and decorate with slices of candied fruit. Between the fruit, snip the cake with a pair of scissors. Sprinkle the cuts with caster sugar. Bake in a hot oven for $\frac{3}{4}$–1 hour or until golden brown.

BUNS

Pan Dulce
Mexican Fairy Cakes

These small buns are usually served for breakfast or, indeed, any time of day as a snack with a glass of white coffee. This recipe will produce 12 buns.

3 eggs	50 g (2 oz) flour
115 g (4 oz) sugar	25 g (1 oz) raisins
1 teaspoon ground cinnamon	Grated peel of 1 orange
Vanilla essence	Caster sugar

Separate the eggs and beat the yolks with the sugar, cinnamon and a few drops of vanilla essence until lemon-coloured. Add the stiffly beaten egg whites and quickly beat in the flour to which the raisins and orange peel have been added. Butter a patty tin and pour spoonfuls of the mixture into the individual cups. Sprinkle a little caster sugar over the top of each bun. Bake in a moderate oven for 15–20 minutes when the buns should be lightly browned.

Soletas
Sponge Fingers

These light sponge fingers are useful as a basis for trifles or to accompany a fruit salad or other dessert.

6 eggs
100 g (4 oz) sugar

150 g (6 oz) flour
50 g (2 oz) caster sugar

Beat the yolks with the sugar until they flow off the spoon in a ribbon. Add the flour bit by bit, then fold in the stiffly beaten egg whites. Squeeze the mixture through a forcing bag (or through a small hole pierced in the corner of a plastic bag) on to a baking-tray covered with greaseproof paper. Sprinkle with caster sugar and bake in a moderate oven for 15–20 minutes.

Bollitos de la Abuela
Grandmother's Buns

250 g (9 oz) flour
¼ teaspoon salt
1 tablespoon baking powder
4 tablespoons sugar
Grated rind of half a lemon

1 tablespoon butter
2 eggs
2 drops vanilla essence
½ cup milk

Sieve together the flour, salt and baking powder and add the sugar and lemon rind. Rub in the butter, then add the eggs, vanilla and enough milk to form a thick dropping consistency. Put spoonfuls of the mixture on to a greased patty-tin and bake in a hot oven for 20 minutes.

Bollos de Mantequilla
Butter Buns

Rich, vanilla-flavoured buns.

250 g (9 oz) butter
20 drops vanilla essence
3 egg yolks

300 g (10½ oz) flour
1 tablespoon baking powder
60 g (2 oz) sugar

Cream the butter, vanilla and egg yolks together in a bowl with a wooden spatula. Add the flour, sifted with the baking powder, and the sugar and mix till a smooth paste is formed. Cut into pieces the size of a lemon. Shape these in the hands and press down with the thumb in the centre. Place on greased trays in a moderate oven for 20 minutes.

BISCUITS

Besos
Kisses

150 g (6 oz) flour
100 g (4 oz) butter
4 egg yolks

100 g (4 oz) sugar
Warm jam for spreading
Icing sugar

Make a well in the centre of the flour and place in it the melted butter, egg yolks and sugar. Mix well until a dough is formed. Roll out to 1½ cm (½ in) thick. Cut into small biscuits with a pastry cutter and place on a greased baking-tray. Bake in a moderate oven for 10–15 minutes. Remove from the heat. Spread jam over one biscuit, place another on top and sprinkle with icing sugar.

Marquesitas
Marquess Biscuits

Crunchy biscuits with an almond topping.

5 eggs	85 g (3 oz) flour
75 g (2½ oz) sugar	50 g (2 oz) blanched almonds

Beat 5 egg yolks and one white together until they are stiff. Add the sugar and continue beating until the mixture is thick. Fold in the flour and finally the remaining egg whites, stiffly beaten. Roll out the mixture, cut into rounds with a pastry cutter, place on trays covered with greaseproof paper. Sprinkle with the finely chopped almonds and bake in a moderate oven for 8 minutes.

Crocantes
Crunchies

500 g (1 lb 2 oz) flour	150 g (5½ oz) butter
15 g (½ oz) baking powder	4 eggs
175 g (6 oz) sugar	

Pour the flour and baking powder on to a board, making a well in the centre. In this place the sugar, butter in small knobs and the eggs. Mix lightly with the hands. Divide into two parts and spread over buttered greaseproof paper on baking-trays. Brush with yolk of egg and place in a moderate oven for 25 minutes. Cut into small squares whilst hot.

Galletitas Monjitas
Nuns' Biscuits

100 g (4 oz) almonds	200 g (7 oz) butter
100 g (4 oz) icing sugar	4 egg yolks
300 g (11 oz) flour	

Toast the unblanched almonds in a little butter and put in a pan with the sugar. When this has gone a good caramel colour empty on to a buttered plate. When it has cooled grind till perfectly smooth. Place the flour on a board and pour the warm melted butter, the sugar and almond paste and the egg yolks into a well in the centre. Mix well with the hands or a wooden spatula and roll out to ½ cm (¼ in) thick. Cut into biscuits with a pastry cutter. Arrange on a baking-tray, brush with egg and cook in a moderate oven for 10 minutes.

Polvorones de Cacahuate
Peanut Biscuits

225 g (8 oz) peanuts
225 g (8 oz) flour

225 g (8 oz) icing sugar
225 g (8 oz) lard

Grind the peanuts in an electric coffee-mill. Sift the flour into a mound and make a well in the centre. Add the sugar, the ground peanuts and the refrigerated lard cut into pieces the size of a pea. Rub in the fat as in making pastry and mix the ingredients thoroughly. Shape the dough into cylindrical rolls, then slice and roll each slice into a small ball. Place the balls with room to spread on a baking-tray and bake in a hot oven for 8–10 minutes.

Sweets

Pasta de Almendra
Marzipan

150 g (6 oz) almonds   250 g (9 oz) sugar
1 egg white

Soak the almonds overnight in cold water. Remove the skins and spread to dry on a dish cloth. Grind the almonds with the egg white in a pestle and mortar or in the electric blender. Boil the sugar in a cup of water until a little forms a thread when taken from the pan. Remove from the heat, add the almonds and beat until the mixture goes very thick. Put on a plate to cool. Once cool, grind again until a very smooth paste is formed. Add colouring as desired and shape into animals, people or stars, etc. by hand or in dampened wooden moulds. Place the moulded marzipan sweets on a rack to dry and air. They may then be stored in a jar.

Cajeta
Milk Toffee

A speciality from Celaya in Guanajuato, made from goats' milk and sugar with a texture rather like fudge.

¼ teaspoon baking powder   1 litre (1¾ pints) goats' milk
1 litre (1¾ pints) cows' milk   500 g (1 lb 2 oz) sugar
10 g (¼–½ oz) cornflour

Dissolve the baking powder in 1 cup of cows' milk and the cornflour in another cup of cows' milk. Bring the rest of the milk to the boil and then add the cows' milk solutions. Add the sugar and continue cooking, stirring constantly until the mixture goes thick and the bottom of the pan can be seen. Pour into a baking-tray and cut into squares whilst still warm.

Dulces de Nuez Oscuros
Walnut Brittle

500 g (1 *lb* 2 *oz*) *unrefined*   ¼ *litre* (½ *pint*) *water*
  brown sugar   150 g (5½ *oz*) *shelled walnuts*

Boil the brown sugar in the water until a little poured on to a plate will form into a soft ball. Remove from the flame and beat till thick. Mix in the chopped walnuts. Drop table-spoons of the mixture on to sheets of waxed paper. Leave to spread out and cool.

Membrillate
Quince *Ate*

Ate or fruit cheese is quite delicious on its own but is especially so after a meal with a slice of soft cheese such as Port Salut. Quince *ate* is a personal favourite, having a sweet but sharp flavour.

1 *kg* (2¼ *lb*) *quinces*   1 *kg* (2¼ *lb*) *sugar*

Peel and core the quinces and soak them briefly in salt water. Soak the cores for 2 hours in 1½ cups of fresh water. Rinse the quinces well and boil in a little water till tender. Cool and grind in the electric blender. Sieve. Boil the sugar in ¼ litre (½ pint) water until a little poured on to a plate forms a soft ball. Add the sieved quince and, when it comes to the boil, the strained water from the soaked cores. Continue simmering gently till a little dropped on to a plate can be lifted off cleanly when cool. Pour into a deep lined baking-tray and when it cools and forms a solid jelly, turn out and cut in slices.

Camotes
Sweet Potato Sweets

The town of Puebla abounds in old-fashioned confectionery shops specifically selling *camotes*, a tasty sweet with a slightly floury texture due to the sweet potatoes which are their main ingredient.

500 g (1 lb 2 oz) sweet potatoes	*250 g (9 oz) sugar to glaze*
250 g (9 oz) sugar	*the sweets*

Peel and boil the sweet potatoes in water to cover until tender (about 30 minutes). Boil 250 g (9 oz) sugar in ¼ litre (½ pint) water till a little dropped on a plate forms a firm ball. Sieve the mashed sweet potato and add to the sugar syrup. Simmer until the mixture forms a paste. Remove from the heat and beat until cool. Roll small pieces of the paste into sticks, the size of a large chip. Place them on a board covered with greaseproof paper, and allow to dry out in the sun. The following day brush the *camotes* with a glaze made by boiling 250 g (9 oz) sugar in ¼ litre (½ pint) water, until a little poured off the spoon on to a plate forms a thick thread. Wrap the individual sweets in waxed paper.

Puchas de Canela
Cinnamon Rings

Pinch of saltpetre	*Pinch of salt*
6 tablespoons orange juice	*Orange blossom water*
6 egg yolks	*200 g (7 oz) sugar*
Flour as necessary	*2 tablespoons ground*
150 g (5½ oz) lard	*cinnamon*

M.C.T.—8

Dissolve the saltpetre in the orange juice. Beat the egg yolks and add enough sifted flour bit by bit to make a dough. Add a few drops of cold melted lard, the strained orange juice, a pinch of salt and a tablespoon of orange blossom water. Knead the dough until smooth. Leave to rest for an hour, then form the dough into small rings. Fry them in hot lard; dip them in a syrup made by boiling the sugar in a $\frac{1}{4}$ cup of water until it spins a fine thread, then left to cool. Dust with plenty of cinnamon.

Drinks

HOT DRINKS

Café de Olla
Pot Coffee

Mexican coffee is some of the best in the world, being grown in the mountainous regions where *café de olla* is sold at stalls in all the villages, often laced with *mescal* or cane spirit against the early morning cold.

150 g (6 oz) *soft brown sugar*   2 *tablespoons finely ground*
½ *litre* (1 *pint*) *water*   *coffee*
1 *stick cinnamon*

Heat the sugar in the water in a tall earthenware pot (if available). When it has dissolved, add the cinnamon and leave to simmer for a few minutes. Remove from the heat, add the coffee, stir well, cover the pot and leave to settle. Strain into small earthenware mugs. Add a sliver of lemon peel if desired.

Chocolate en Leche
Hot Chocolate

Chocolate is handmade in Mexico as well as being produced commercially. The cocoa bean is ground on a *metate* (a large flat rectangular grinding stone with a long rolling-pin-shaped stone for grinding) with a fire burning under it. Sugar, cinnamon and ground almonds are added and hard-boiled egg yolks to make it froth up when beaten with a *molinillo*.

To make Mexican hot chocolate in Britain, you will need:

2 *blanched almonds*
12 *teaspoons cocoa powder*
4 *dessertspoons sugar*

2 *teaspoons cinnamon*
1 *hard-boiled egg yolk*
1½ *litres (3 pints) milk*

Grind the almonds very finely and mix with the cocoa powder, sugar, cinnamon and crushed egg yolk. Mix with a little of the milk. Put the rest of the milk to boil in a tall earthenware pot or saucepan. When it begins to climb up the sides add the cocoa mixture. Boil over a very low light for 5 minutes, whipping with a *molinillo* or an egg whisk till it froths. Serve very hot in earthenware mugs.

Té de Manzanilla
Camomile Tea

Camomile tea is highly favoured in Mexico. It is refreshing and reputedly calms the nerves. A good bedtime drink.

1 *litre (1¾ pints) water*
1 *handful camomile flowers*
  (*with stalks and leaves if*
  fresh flowers are available)

4 *dessertspoons soft brown*
  sugar

Boil all the ingredients together gently for 5–10 minutes. Leave to infuse, then strain the tea into earthenware cups.

Atole
Atole

Atole is a thick sustaining drink made with cornflour or oatmeal.

75 *g (2½ oz) cornflour or*
  poridge oats
½ *litre (1 pint) water*

1 *stick cinnamon*
200 *g (7 oz) sugar*
1 *litre (1¾ pints) milk*

Dissolve the cornflour in the water, add the cinnamon and simmer gently until it begins to thicken. Add the sugar and the milk and leave to boil, stirring constantly with a wooden spoon, until as thick as cream. Serve piping hot as a bedtime drink, to warm up on cold days or as an accompaniment to *tamales*.

Champurrado
Champurrado

200 g (7 oz) cornflour
1½ litres (3 pints) water

250 g (9 oz) unrefined brown
    sugar
75 g (2½ oz) chocolate

Dissolve the cornflour in the water and simmer until thick, stirring constantly with a wooden spoon. Add the brown sugar and the chocolate and whip with a chocolate beater or egg whisk until well blended. Boil up once more and serve.

COLD DRINKS

Licuados
Fruit Shakes

Most Mexican meals are washed down with a fruit shake made in the blender: melon, paw-paw, water-melon or carrots cut into chunks and blended; strawberries and bananas mixed with milk; and oranges squeezed. A raw egg is often added, especially at breakfast time, the orange juice being whisked with the egg in the blender.

Horchata
Horchata

Horchata is a refreshing drink with body to it, made from melon seeds. It is the traditional accompaniment to *puchero* (see p. 78).

250 g (9 oz) melon seeds   Grated peel of 1 lemon
2 litres (3½ pints) water   Ice
250 g (9 oz) sugar

Grind the melon seeds and add the water, sugar and the
grated lemon peel. Allow to stand for 5 hours, strain through
a damp cloth and serve in tall glasses on crushed ice.

ALCOHOLIC DRINKS

Beer, drunk with a squeeze of lemon and a sprinkle of salt,
is the great favourite in Mexico, being most refreshing in the
hot weather. Here are some other traditional alcoholic
drinks which can be made in Britain.

Sangría
Sangría

½ litre (1 pint) red wine   450 g (1 lb) sugar
½ litre (1 pint) water   4 tablespoons lemon juice
1 litre (2 pints) orange juice Ice

Dissolve the sugar in the water and combine with the other
liquids. Serve in tall gasses with crushed ice.

Margarita
Margarita Cocktail

Tequila is Mexico's best-known alcoholic drink and is taken
with a quarter of lemon in one hand and a dab of salt on
the back of the other. Lick the salt, take a bite on the lemon
and swallow a liqueur glass full of tequila in one gulp. The
less venturesome may prefer the Margarita cocktail which is
made as follows:

½ litre (1 pint) tequila   Soda water to taste
4 lemons   Crushed ice
250 g (8 oz) sugar

Squeeze the lemons and dissolve the juice with the sugar, add the tequila and mix well. Pour a little into tall glasses with crushed ice and top up with soda water to taste.

Coco Fizz
Gin and Coconut Milk Cocktail

A very refreshing cocktail served in coconut shells at Acapulco.

½ litre (1 pint) gin
½ litre (1 pint) coconut milk
4 tablespoons sugar

2 lemons
Soda water

Mix the gin, coconut milk, sugar and lemon juice in a cocktail shaker with ice. Fill the glasses almost full, topping up with soda water.

Rompope
Rompope

Akin to Advocaat, this drink can be bottled and kept for a long time.

½ litre (1 pint) rum
2 litres (4 pints) milk
1 kg (2 lb) sugar

16 egg yolks
1 vanilla pod

Boil the milk, leave to cool and add the sugar and vanilla. Re-heat and boil gently for 20 minutes. Remove from the heat and leave to cool. Beat the egg yolks to the ribbon (3–4 minutes' continuous beating: the eggs should run from the spoon held above the basin in a broad ribbon). Add the cooled milk and rum little by little. Cover the receptacle until the foam has died down. Strain and bottle.

Table of Weights and Measures

Most of the recipes in the book give quantities in kilos and grams followed by the nearest round figure equivalent in pounds and ounces. If you are doubling or halving the quantities, it is wiser to take the kilo measure as your base and convert to pounds and ounces using the following table.

1 kg	$2\frac{1}{4}$ lb
900 g	2 lb
800 g	1 lb 12 oz
750 g	1 lb 10 oz
700 g	1 lb 9 oz
600 g	1 lb 5 oz
500 g	1 lb 2 oz
400 g	14 oz
300 g	$10\frac{1}{2}$ oz
250 g	9 oz
200 g	7 oz
100 g	$3\frac{1}{2}$ oz
50 g	$1\frac{3}{4}$ oz
25 g	1 oz
15 g	$\frac{1}{2}$ oz
10 g	$\frac{1}{3}$ oz

Table of Oven Heats

	Electricity	Gas
very slow	225F (110C)	$\frac{1}{4}$
very slow	250F (120C)	$\frac{1}{2}$
slow	275F (140C)	1
slow	300F (150C)	2
moderate	325F (160C)	3
moderate	350F (180C)	4
fairly hot	375F (190C)	5
fairly hot	400F (200C)	6
hot	425F (220C)	7
very hot	450F (230C)	8
very hot	475F (240C)	9

Stockists of Mexican Foods and Products

Minza, cornmeal flour for making tortillas, is stocked by:

International & American Food Centre, 354 Coombe Lane, West Wimbledon, London SW20. Tel. 01-946 5478

Panzers Delicatessen, 13/19 Circus Rd., St. John's Wood, London NW8. Tel. 01-722 8596

Fresh coriander leaf may be bought at Asian and Greek greengrocers around London, such as the 5 Continents Store, Westbourne Grove, London. Beans, chiles and fresh fruits such as mangoes and paw-paws can also be bought at similar stores.

Stockists of tinned Mexican products include:

Jacksons of Piccadilly, 172 Piccadilly, London W1. Tel. 01-493 1033

Jacksons of Sloane St., 6a Sloane St., London SW1. Tel. 01-235 9233

Mr. Christian's Delicatessen, 11 Elgin Crescent, London W11. Tel. 01-229 0501

Wine & Food Centre, 196 Kensington High St., London W8

John Barker & Co., Kensington High St., London W8

Harrods Ltd., Food Halls, Knightsbridge, London SW3. Tel. 01-730 1234

Mexican Products Ltd., 10 Jeffries Passage, Guildford, Surrey. Tel. Guildford 75776

Index

Also available from Magnum Books

Jean Conil

THE MAGNUM COOKBOOK

The Magnum Cookbook is a must for all serious cooks. It contains a wide variety of recipes ranging from the basic to exotic, as well as exciting recipes for special occasions. Roast beef and Yorkshire pudding and a host of other traditional English recipes are included.

Master Chef Jean Conil's experience as a chef and nutritionist has enabled him to write a comprehensive book covering all aspects of cookery. He outlines the basic 'do's' and 'don'ts' of which every cook should be aware; a knowledge which he hopes will give confidence and inspiration to develop new ideas in the kitchen.

Jean Conil has had a varied career as chef, restauranteur, author and teacher. He broadcasts regularly on LBC and has recently been appearing on BBC TV's 'Nationwide' programme.

Jan Hopcraft

COOKING TODAY, EATING TOMORROW

Do you like to cook for your friends but always find yourself too rushed to enjoy it? This bestselling cookery book is designed for busy people. The recipes are clearly presented in the form of menus for dinner, lunch and fork supper parties. No menu contains more than one dish which has to be made from start to finish on the actual day. Each recipe has been specially designed to cut right down on time spent in the kitchen at the last minute, so that you can enjoy more time with your guests.

ENTERTAINING ON A BUDGET

A practical guide to tempting yet inexpensive meals for entertaining. Jan Hopcraft demonstrates that lashings of wine and cream are not essential for a first-class meal. She uses cider and a wide range of herbs and spices to transform simple ingredients into delicious and exciting dishes. These imaginative recipes include totally new ideas as well as traditional dishes and advice on cutting costs. Many dishes can be prepared in advance, making this an essential cookery book for those who have to economise on time as well as cost.

Carolyn McCrum

THE SOUP BOOK

Soup is a versatile food suitable for all occasions.
A delicate consommé will make a fine start to a rich
meal; an iced soup is wonderfully refreshing on a
summer's day; and a meat soup can satisfy the heartiest
appetite as a complete meal on a winter's night.

In **The Soup Book** Carolyn McCrum explains the
basic methods and essential equipment for stock and
soup-making. There are many recipes ranging from
simple soups that can be prepared in minutes to
elaborate soups like the famed Bouillabaise, Pot-au-
Feu and Gazpacho. Favourite soups are included as
well as new ideas, such as Iced Coconut and
Aubergine Soup. The recipes are arranged practically
for particular occasions; time-saving soups, cool
summer soups, and main course soups for family
suppers.

The Soup Book will persuade you that the soup you
make yourself is infinitely superior to the processed
kind: it is delicious, nourishing, wonderfully versatile
and a pleasure to prepare.

Rosemary Stark

THE MIRACLE COOKBOOK

Most of us experience at some time or other that sinking feeling when guests turn up unexpectedly for a meal. Panic no more, for Rosemary Stark comes to the rescue with a wealth of ideas for improvisation in the kitchen. By adding an extra course or expanding what's to hand with goodies from the store cupboard, you can even stretch two pork chops between four people.

The Miracle Cookbook has an invaluable guide to storing food so that in a crisis you need only look through the Index of Ingredients to come up with a meal that will please your guests and surprise you at your own capability.

Other non-fiction available from Magnum Books

These and other Magnum Books are available at your bookshop or newsagent. In case of difficulties orders may be sent to :

> Magnum Books
> Cash Sales Department
> P.O. Box 11
> Falmouth
> Cornwall TR10 109EN

Please send cheque or postal order, no currency, for purchase price quoted and allow the following for postage and packing:

U.K. 19p for the first book plus 9p per copy for each additional book ordered, to a maximum of 75p.

B.F.P.O. & Eire 19p for the first book plus 9p per copy for the next 6 books, thereafter 3p per book.

Overseas customers 20p for the first book and 10p per copy for each additional book.

While every effort is made to keep prices low, it is sometimes necessary to increase prices at short notice. Magnum Books reserve the right to show new retail prices on covers which may differ from those previously advertised in the text or elsewhere.